I0632445

Dehydrated
& Delicious

The Complete Book on Dehydrating Meats, Fruits, Vegetables, Herbs, Flowers, Yogurt and more!

by **Ron Popeil**
and John May

Printed in the United States of America

For inquiries contact:

Dehydrator Products
P.O. Box 4120
Carlsbad, CA 92018

TABLE OF CONTENTS

CHAPTER 1

GETTING STARTED

CHAPTER 2

DELICIOUS FRUITS

CHAPTER 3

WONDERFUL VEGETABLES

TABLE OF CONTENTS

CHAPTER 4

MEMORABLE JERKY

CHAPTER 5

HERBS, POTPOURRI, AND DRY FLOWERS

TABLE OF CONTENTS

CHAPTER 6

YOGURT MADE AT HOME

CHAPTER 7

FACTS ABOUT STORING

First, I want to thank you for your interest in our book, *Dehydrated & Delicious*. As you may know from my television program, I've been involved with hundreds of time and money saving products over the years. The Ronco Electric Food Dehydrator is certainly one of my favorites. As of this writing, I'm selling more Electric Food Dehydrator and Beef Jerky Machines than anyone else in the world. And for good reason — it's a great product!

Good food and good cooking have always been important to me in my life. With this book full of ideas and recipes, you, too, can enjoy *even more* money-saving, natural and delicious dehydrated foods.

I sincerely wish you all good food and good fun. Thanks again.

Ron Popeil, President
Ronco, Inc.

Note to Readers: We'd like to hear from you. Call us with your comments and questions at 1-800-688-0998.

CHAPTER 1

GETTING STARTED

INTRODUCTION TO DRYING

Drying fruits, vegetables, and meats will enable you to create some of the tastiest and convenient ready to eat snacks that everybody in the family can enjoy. Not only will they be some of the best tasting snacks, but also less expensive than store purchased snacks. Dehydrated foods make wonderful additions in favorite recipes for casseroles, soups, stews, and salads. Dried fruits and berries are used to make excellent compotes and sauces.

Drying is appealing because fruits and vegetables can be eaten year round. Using them is convenient, relatively simple and requires little equipment. The Ronco Electric Food Dehydrator is the only piece of equipment you need. Only minimal storage space is needed for dried food.

Dried foods used a short time after dehydration are delicious and have an equally appealing flavor as fresh fruits and vegetables. Dehydrated fruits will stay delicious for many months. For optimum flavor they are made just a few weeks before expected use. Vegetables are most flavorful when eaten within a month from the time they were dried.

Beef, fish, and other types of jerky are dried with a minimum of effort. Home dried jerky is superb tasting and far less expensive than store purchased.

The Ronco Electric Food Dehydrator has other uses; yogurt, dried herbs, flowers and potpourri can all be done easily.

Drying requires a method of heating food to remove the moisture through evaporation. Moisture is drawn from the food as warm air moves over and around it. The movement of air around the food is the key to drying.

Drying is a relatively simple process, but there are a number of recommended techniques. You may need to use a "trial and error" approach to find the drying procedure which works best for a particular situation. Fruits and vegetables can be dried in pieces or pureed and dried in a thin sheet called "leather" or fruit roll up.

Before drying is started, food must be given a pretreatment to preserve the taste, texture, and nutrients. The typical pretreatments include coating fruit with an anti-oxidant, sulfuring, or steam blanching. Vegetables are steam blanched or boiled and meats are treated with salt solutions.

During the drying process, from preparation to storage and eating, precaution should be taken to protect food from insects and food spoilers. Care should be taken so only food grade materials come into contact with the food. Properly dried fruits and vegetables do not have enough moisture content to support organisms that create spoilage. Drying creates an environment that does allow molds, yeast and bacteria to grow.

Foods like vegetables with low acid content have enzymes which speed up the spoilage process. Temperatures used for drying will make the enzymes inactive, but they do not kill them.

Precooking is a method that can be used to not only destroy the enzymes but also to help maintain the foods original texture, color, and flavor.

The goal of drying is to take away the water content of foods so spoiling organisms can not grow and multiply. Home dried foods should have only 5 to 20 percent of their original water content. Vegetables usually only have 5 to 10 percent water and fruits may have a higher water content (10 to 20 percent) because the sugar in them aids in the preserving.

WHEN IS THE FOOD "DRY"
The most common method used to determine if the food is dry is to sample the food pieces. It is best to taste and feel a small sample of the pieces. The food texture is a key to determining whether it is sufficiently dry. Generally, fruit that is dry, feels dry and leathery outside and moist inside. Fruit should feel pliable and will have a color characteristic of the fresh fruit.

Vegetables should be brittle and slightly tough. When they are dry they generally will rattle on the trays.   The color should be characteristic of the fresh vegetable.

Meats will be hard and crack when they are bent but should not break.   Each chapter in this book contains a section with instructions for drying the different food types and how to check for dryness.

Weighing the food is a popular and helpful way to determine whether the food is sufficiently dry.   You simply weigh the food before it is dried.   It should weigh about 10 to 20 percent of its weight after drying.

A note about the terminology: According to the USDA, "Dehydration" means that all water is removed except for 2.5 to 4 percent.   Only commercially prepared foods are able to reach this level of dryness.   The home drying process is only able to reduce the water content to 5 to 20 percent which is what the USDA terms as "dried".   In this book we will use the terms "dehydration",   "drying"   and   "dried" interchangeable to mean foods with 5 to 20 percent water content.

Food can be dried in the sun, in an oven, or in a dehydrator.   The Ronco Electric Food Dehydrator is by far the easiest and most convenient to use. Dehydrators typically produce a better end product especially when working with foods that have high moisture content.

Home dehydrators are able to keep foods at a relatively uniform temperature. Home dryers require less energy so are less expensive to use. They also require a minimum of attention, so your time is not spent watching over the drying process.

There are no absolute amounts of time it takes to dry each type of food. Later in this book you will find charts with suggested drying times. They are guidelines and approximate the usual drying time. There are many variables which can affect drying time. The type of food, the thickness it is cut, size of batch, moisture content, type of pretreatment, humidity, altitude, etc. can all affect dehydrating times.

Letting food dry too long is a common mistake. When the food is heated from the dryer it will be soft and pliable. In order to test it you must take it out of the dryer and allow it to cool. A good rule of thumb is to take a sample of food out of the dryer before you think it is done to test it. You'll find once it has been allowed to cool, many of the pieces are finished. Remove pieces as they dry rather than wait for the whole batch to dry.

Separate the finished food from that which needs more time. Simply put back any pieces that are too moist so they can dry some more.

Checking the food occasionally after it has been allowed to dry for awhile is an important step. It's helpful to put a note next to the dehydrator with the time the drying process started and the last time you checked it. This gives you a good idea of when to check your batch again and helps you perfect your drying methods to a science.

Food on drying trays should be rotated during the drying process. The trays nearest the bottom are exposed to the hottest, driest air, and will dry more rapidly.

By paying attention to the details you will achieve high quality dried foods. First begin with only the best quality food. By using high quality food you will get high quality dried food. Even though the food is dried it retains its flavor. Use ripe, sweet fruit, and fresh vegetables. You can taste the difference when quality produce is used for drying. Many people report they can taste the difference between fruits and vegetables that were purchased at the store and dried; and food from the home garden that was dried.

SELECTING AND HANDLING FOODS FOR DRYING

SELECTING FOODS
Use the same criteria for selecting fruits and vegetables for drying as you would for selecting produce to be eaten fresh.   The fruits and vegetables should be chosen when they are as close to peak color, taste, and freshness as possible.   Ideally you would use produce that was picked the same day you begin the drying process.

The drying process will not cover up imperfections in your produce quality.   The quality you start with determines the quality you get at the end.   The drying process simply preserves the quality of the produce at the time it was dried.

Avoid using produce that has been damaged, bruised or spoiled slightly because they are more likely to spoil.   An entire batch can be ruined by even the slightest bit of decay.

HANDLING FOOD AFTER HARVEST
By making sure you harvest the highest quality produce you are half way to making high quality dried food.   How you handle the food after harvest is   equally important.

Immediately cool all the harvested produce. Even at room temperature fruits and vegetables begin to deteriorate quickly. By placing the food in cold storage as soon as possible you will slow the loss of quality. Ideal temperature to keep produce fresh is between 32 and 40 degrees F. In addition to storing in the refrigerator, other ways to cool produce is to cover with cracked ice, or immerse in ice water. The key to getting the highest quality tasting foods is to immediately slow the spoilage process and preserve the freshest flavor and texture possible.

KEEPING PIECES UNIFORM IN SIZE

When cutting each slice of food, uniformity is important. Keep each piece of food as close to the same size as possible. The size of the food pieces determine how long it takes to dry. If food pieces are the same size they will dry at the same rate.

The pieces should each be cut about 1/8 to 1/4 inch thick. Most dried fruits and vegetables taste great with their peelings, so peel if you want, but it is optional. Cut out all bad spots or bruises.

The food should be put on the dehydrator trays without any overlapping. A good rule of thumb is to use 3/4 of the tray surface area. This allows the air to circulate freely and helps achieve uniform drying in your batch. As the food dries and shrinks it will free up space on the trays.

You can then combine contents on the trays to gain additional space, and to add more food to the drying process. When drying shredded food, turn and gently stir the pieces regularly for fast, even drying. If drying herbs use your Ronco Herb Screens for best results. Use the Ronco Fruit Roll Trays for your fruit leathers and roll ups.

NUTRIENT RETENTION IN DRIED FOODS

By promptly preparing and drying foods after they are harvested you are able to preserve vitamins and minerals. As with all methods of food preservation, there is some loss of nutrients with dried foods.

During the preparation and drying process certain vitamins will be preserved and others reduced by varying degrees. Generally the nutritional value of dried foods is about the same as frozen food.

Vitamins A and C will be lost primarily during the pretreating process when they are boiled or steamed. Vitamin A diminishes quickly if food is dried in the sun. Drying with a dehydrator will help preserve Vitamin A, but over time Vitamin A is lost in dried foods.

The drying process has a varied affect on the B Vitamins. Niacin is retained; Riboflavin can be preserved if the food is stored in a dark place.

Thiamine is destroyed during sulfuring and by the heat used during drying.

Vitamin C is preserved during the sulfuring process which is used to retain color and slow spoilage.

Proteins and carbohydrates are not greatly destroyed by the drying process. In fact, carbohydrates can actually be made more readily available for digestion by drying. The body can more efficiently digest carbohydrates from dehydrated food.

Sugars remain in the food after the water is removed, leaving the sugar concentrated. If you are counting calories, remember the dried fruit weighs less, so it takes more to fill you up. Each ounce of dried fruit will have as many calories as several times its weight in fresh fruit.

Minerals are generally not destroyed by drying, but some are lost by steaming and boiling during blanching.

By using the freshest food possible and by careful blanching, you can produce nutritional dried food that not only tastes great but is good for you.

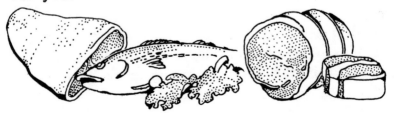

CONDITIONING, STORING, AND PACKAGING

CONDITIONING THE FOOD AFTER DRYING

Even after careful drying, all the individual pieces of food may not be equally dry. Some may have more moisture content than other pieces. To equalize the moisture in the batch and insure that all pieces are sufficiently dry you want to condition the batch before storing.

Conditioning means placing the food in an enamel or plastic container (do not use metal) to allow it to dry further. The container should be covered to protect it from insects and dust, but it should not be airtight. You want to have air circulation to continue moisture evaporation.

Stir the food once or twice each day for up to two weeks. When the batch is evenly dried, place the food in the oven preheated at 175 degrees F. Heat for 10 to 15 minutes. Allow the batch to cool before packaging.

STORING DRIED FOOD

To keep the food nutritious and fresh tasting, store it in a cool dark area. Dried food can be kept at room temperature but the best tasting dried foods are stored at temperatures below 60 degrees F.

PACKAGING DRIED FOOD

When the food has cooled thoroughly, you can begin packaging it. Vacuum food sealers are optimal if you have one. If not, plastic ziplock bags will work well if you squeeze out the extra air.

If your food was sun dried or exposed to open air for more than a short period of time, you may want to protect it from insect infestation. Freezing the food for 48 hours will destroy any possible insect infestation.

To preserve the highest quality of food, it should also be protected from heat, moisture, light, and of course from pests.

Food stored in clear plastic bags will be damaged by light unless the bags are placed in a container which does not allow exposure to light.

A few days after storing, check for moisture in the bags. If you see moisture, it means the food was not dry enough.

You should check for moisture in the packages for two weeks. If caught in time any moist food can be put back in the dehydrator and saved by additional drying.

It is a good idea to package food in small quantities that can be eaten at one time. Store consistent amounts in each package you make.

Three to four cups of dried food per package is good.

LABEL YOUR DRIED FOOD

Be sure to label all your packages. It is a good idea to write the date you packed the food, what it is, how much it weighs, and what you intended to make with it. It is fun to also include any unique or personal data on the label. For instance; who helped with the drying or packaging process, how the process went, if it was a special occasion, a family member's favorite food, etc.

PRETREATMENT AND PREPARATION TECHNIQUES

Most fruits and vegetables need some type of pretreatment or cooking before they can be dried. Fruits and vegetables contain enzymes which are responsible for changes in the flavor and color as it ripens. The purpose of pretreating produce before drying it is to slow the enzyme process to maintain the best possible flavor and color.

PRETREATING FRUITS
Sulfuring is a pretreatment to prevent foods from darkening during the drying and storage process. Vitamins A and C are preserved by sulfuring. Fruits that are not sulfured tend to get moldy, lose their flavor, and be more readily attacked by insects than sulfur treated fruits.

Sulfuring does destroy thiamine. However, fruits are not considered an important source of thiamine.

The best method of sulfuring is to treat the foods with burning sulfur fumes in a box. This treatment must be done outside because the smoke and fumes will be objectionable indoors.
A sulfuring box can be easily constructed using cardboard. A more permanent box can be constructed out of wood.

HOW TO SULFUR

As previously mentioned, fruit treated with sulfur should also be dried outdoors.

Here are the steps for sulfuring with fumes:

1. Place the cut fruit on wooden trays in a single layer with cut surfaces facing up. Sulfur up to four trays at a time.

2. Trays should be stacked three inches apart and stacked on wood blocks at each corner of the tray. The bottom tray should be placed on concrete blocks or bricks.

3. The trays should be made of wood and should not have any metal on them at all. The trays should have narrow lathing strips that allow the air and fumes to circulate freely around the food.

4. You'll need a heavy cardboard or wooden box that covers the fruit trays. The box will not have a top and will be placed upside down over the trays so the ground will act as the floor of the box. Allow for 2 inches of clearance on the sides of your wooden trays. Allow for six inches between the top tray and the box. You'll need 12 inches total clearance between the front of the trays and the box for room to put the sulfuring dish next to the trays.

5.   At the bottom, near one corner of the box, cut out a slot one inch high by six inches wide. This will allow air to enter the box. Near the top of the opposite corner of the box, make a hole about one quarter inch in diameter or about the size of a pencil. This hole helps with circulation of air flow to keep the sulfur burning.

6. Use one tablespoon of Sulfur Flowers (U.S.P. standard) for each pound of fruit. Place the sulfur in a baking tray and put it in front of the wooden trays. The baking tray must not be made of metal and should be perfectly clean before each use.

7. Light the sulfur and place the box over the stack of trays. Make sure the fumes do not escape between the ground and the box by building dirt around the box or using towels to trap in the fumes.

8.   Caution should always be used when lifting the box to check on the fruit. Reach across the top of the box, and tilt the box toward you on its side. Allow the fumes to escape in the direction opposite you. It takes approximately 15 minutes for the sulfur to burn.

9. After the sulfur has started burning, cover both holes in the sulfuring box to keep the box airtight.   Once the box is airtight, simply leave it and let the fumes permeate the fruit.

10. The amount of time it takes to sulfur after the sulfur has finished burning varies according to type of fruit, size of pieces, and other various conditions. Sun dried fruit will take about twice as long as food dried in a home dehydrator.

11. A general rule for small pieces dried in a home dehydrator is 20 to 30 minutes. Small pieces dried in the sun should be sulfured 40 to 60 minutes. Double the amount of time for quartered pieces and double that time for fruit halves.

The fruit will appear bright and glistening when sulfuring is complete. You'll want to use any juice that has collected on the fruit during sulfuring to enhance the fruits flavor during dehydration.

SULFUR DIP SOLUTION
Sulfuring can also be done by dipping fruit into a sodium bisulfite solution. This is an easy and quick method, but many feel it is not very satisfactory. When the fruit is soaked in the solution there is a loss of nutrients, the pieces tend to get water logged, and the sulfur compound does not always penetrate the fruit tissues evenly.

To make a sulfite solution for dipping fruit use one teaspoon of sodium bisulfite per quart of water. Dip the fruit for only two minutes unless the instructions call for longer soaking. Place fruit on paper towels to drain. Dry fruit outdoors.

STEAM SULFUR BLANCHING
To steam blanch the fruit with sulfur use one to two teaspoons of sodium bisulfite in two cups of water. Steam the fruit over the solution for a couple of minutes until the fruit becomes translucent. Dry the fruit outdoors.

It is important to use sodium bisulfite and not sodium bisulfate, which is toxic.

While sulfuring is the most effective pretreatment to hold the color and flavor of fruit, there are other methods that can be used as well. They follow below.

ASCORBIC ACID DIP
Ascorbic acid is Vitamin C and is a very effective anti-oxidant. Drug stores and health food stores carry pure crystalline ascorbic acid. If you have trouble finding a store that sells it, regular Vitamin C tablets in 400-mg or 500-mg doses can be crushed and works equally as well. You can substitute five to six teaspoons of crushed vitamin tablets for each teaspoon of pure crystalline ascorbic acid.

The strength of the ascorbic acid solution depends on the type of fruit being treated. Light colored fruit like apples require a high concentrated solution of 3 teaspoons of pure crystalline ascorbic acid for each cup of water.

Fruit that is not as light colored can be dipped in a less concentrated solution of 1 to 2 teaspoons of pure crystalline ascorbic acid per cup of water.

One cup of ascorbic acid solution can coat about 5 quarts of fruit. Simply sprinkle the solution over the cut pieces of fruit making sure each piece is coated.

SYRUP BLANCHING

Syrup blanching   prevents discoloration, but the
other methods are considered better.   Fruits
treated in syrup tend to be sticky and retain the
sweetness of the syrup.   The flavor of the dried
fruit moves toward a candy-like taste.

The syrup is made by combining 1 cup of sugar
for every cup of water.   Honey and corn syrup
can be substituted for sugar.   Lighter solutions
can be made by combining 1 cup of sweetener
with 2 to 3 cups of water.

Heat and stir the solution until it boils.   Lower
the heat to a simmer, and drop the fruit pieces
into the syrup.   Simmer the fruit for 5 to 15
minutes.   Remove the container from the heat
and let the fruit stand in the syrup for an
additional 10 to 15 minutes.   Use a strainer to
drain the fruit.   The fruit should be allowed to
drain further on paper towels before drying to
remove as much syrup as possible.

STEAM BLANCHING

Steam blanching can also be used   to prevent
oxidation and preserve color and flavor.   Put
water into a steamer or pot with a tight fitting
lid and bring   to a boil.   Place a steam basket or
wire rack in the pot so that the water level will
not touch the fruit.

Put the cut pieces of fruit into the basket or rack. Do not pile the pieces more than 2 inches deep. Close the lid and steam for 3 to 5 minutes.

Steam blanching can also be essential for checking or cracking the tough skins of fruits like grapes, cherries, prunes, plums, berries, etc. The steam is effective in cracking the skins so that moisture can more readily escape during the drying process, thus reducing the drying time.

Fruits and berries with tougher skins may have to be dipped into boiling water in order to crack their tough skins. Usually 30 to 60 seconds is adequate to break the skins. Place the fruit in cold water immediately after removing it from the boiling water. This will prevent further cooking.

MICROWAVE BLANCHING

Your microwave instructions are the best source of directions for blanching in your microwave. This is a great way to pretreat fruit and you can't go wrong with this process. If you don't have instructions for your microwave oven follow these steps:

Blanch one pound of fruit at a time in a very small amount of water. Blanching takes 2 to 6 minutes. Stop the microwave after half the blanching time has expired and check the fruit to make sure the pieces are blanching evenly. Rearrange the pieces if necessary.

OTHER METHODS OF BLANCHING

The above blanching methods are the best ways to prepare fruit for drying. Below are some additional methods for pretreating fruit.

Lemon Juice

Using 1/4 cup of lemon juice to 1 quart of water will create a solution for dipping or blanching that will preserve fruit color.

Salt Water

A salt water dip solution can be made by mixing one to two tablespoons of salt with each quart of water. Soak fruit for 10 to 20 minutes.

Vinegar Dip

Add one tablespoon of vinegar and one tablespoon of salt to each quart of water to create a vinegar and salt dip. Fruit should soak about 10 minutes.

PRETREATMENT OF VEGETABLES

Steam blanching is the most effective method of treating vegetables for drying. Steam blanching is preferred over boiling because nutrients are leeched out when vegetables are placed in water.

Use the same instructions for blanching vegetables as those listed above for blanching fruit. Blanched vegetables will not only retain better flavor and color texture but also require less drying time and less soaking time when rehydrating or refreshing.

CHAPTER 2

DELICIOUS FRUITS

HOME DRYING OF FRUITS

Now you are ready to get started making delightful dried fruit. Have fun and use the following references to make fruit drying easy. You will find the fruits organized in alphabetical order with preparation and pretreatment methods, approximate drying times, how to test if the fruit is dry, and how to refresh or reconstitute each fruit.

Enjoy your dried fruits by themselves or use them to make the tasty recipes at the end of this chapter. Have fun experimenting with the many ways of using deliciously dry fruit.

HOW TO PREPARE, DRY, AND REFRESH FRUITS

APPLES

Preparation: Peel and core, cut into slices or rings about 1/8 thick.

Pretreatment: Sulfur fumes: 45 minutes; steam blanch: 5 minutes, depending on texture.

Drying time: Dehydrator 6 to 12 hours; sun: 3 to 4 days.

Dryness test: Soft, pliable, no moist area in center when cut.

Refreshing: Presoak 1 cup dried apples in 1 1/2 cups hot water until plump and moist. Simmer covered, 15 minutes or until tender.

Storage time: 4 to 6 months at 70 degrees F.

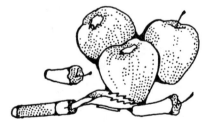

APRICOTS

Preparation: Pit and halve for steam blanch or sulfuring. Leave whole for water blanch, pit and halve after blanching.
Pretreatment: Sulfur fumes: 2 hours; steam blanch: 3 to 4 minutes; water blanch: 4 to 5 minutes.
Drying time: Dehydrator: 24 to 36 hours; sun 2 to 3 days.
Dryness test: Soft, pliable, leathery, with no moist area in center.
Refreshing and preparation: Presoak 1 cup apricots to 1 1/2 cups hot water.
Storage time: 6 to 8 months at 70 degrees F.

BANANAS

Preparation: Peel ripe bananas, and slice evenly 1/4 inch thick.
Pretreatment: Hold 2 to 3 minutes in solution of 1 quart water and 1 teaspoon ascorbic acid, or blanch in heavy syrup for 2 minutes.
Drying time: Dehydrator: 12 to 24 hours; oven: 5 to 6 hours.
Dryness test: Firm, chewy, and leathery texture.
Refreshing : Soak 1 cup bananas in 1 1/2 cups hot water for 2 hours.
Storage time: 2 to 4 months at 70 degrees F.

BERRIES

Preparation: Use firm berries like blueberries, cranberries, elderberries, and currants. Wash and remove stems.

Pretreatment: Plunge prepared berries with tough skins into boiling water for 15 to 30 seconds to crack skins, then into cold water to cool rapidly, and drain. Less tough-skinned varieties may be steam blanched for 30 to 60 seconds or dried without pretreatment.

Drying time: Dehydrator: 6 to 10 hours, depending upon fruit; oven: 2 hours at 120 degree F., then 140 degrees F. about 2 hours more, or until dry; sun: 1 to 2 days.

Dryness test: Hard. No moisture when crushed. Fruits rattle when tray is shaken.

Refreshing: Cover with water and store in refrigerator overnight. To cook, cover with water and simmer until tender.

Storage time: 4 to 6 months at 70 degrees F.

CHERRIES

Preparation: Stem, wash, drain, and pit. Cherries may be halved or left whole.
Pretreatment: If cut and pitted no pretreatment is needed. Dip whole cherries in boiling water to crack skin.
Drying time: Dehydrator: 24 hours; oven: 4 to 6 hours. Start at 120 degrees F. and increase to 145 degrees F.
Dryness test: Leathery and sticky.
Refreshing: Pour 2 cups hot water to 1 cup cherries and soak 2 hours.
Storage time: 8 to 12 months at 70 degrees F.

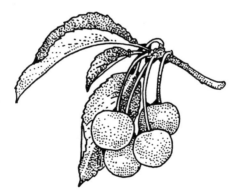

CITRUS PEELS

Varieties best for drying: The peels of citron, grapefruit, kumquat, lemon, lime, orange, tangelo or tangerine are best for drying. Do not dry fruit peels if marked "color added" by grocer.

Preparation: Wash well.   Cut the peel into strips 1 1/2 inches and about 1/16 to 1/8 inch thick. The outer part of the peel has the flavorful oils.   Cut above the white pith which is bitter.

Pretreatment: None.

Drying time: Dehydrator: 8 to 12 hours; sun: 4 to 6 hours.

Dryness test: Crisp.

How to use: Store strips in airtight containers. Dried peelings are twice as flavorful as fresh so use half the amount.   A blender   can be used to make grated peels if desired.

Storage time: 4 to 6 months at 70 degrees F.

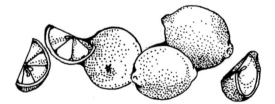

COCONUTS

Selection: Select fresh coconuts that seem to be heavy with milk. Refrigerate coconuts until ready to dehydrate.

Preparation: Pierce eye of the coconut with an ice pick to drain the milk. Strain milk to drink. Use a hammer to crack the middle of the coconut. Steam the shell for 30 to 60 seconds to loosen the coconut meat. Trim the dark outer skin and grate or slice coconut into chunks for drying.

Pretreatment: None

Drying time: Dehydrator: 8 to 10 hours; sun: 1 to 2 days.

Refreshing: Use dry, or soak in water until tender before using in a recipe.

Storage time: 2 to 4 weeks at 70 degrees F.

CRANBERRIES

Selection: Select fresh firm cranberries. Cranberries do not dry as well as other fruits. The large bright red variety or the sweet dark variety dry the best. Cranberries are great when dried as part of a fruit leather recipe.
Preparation: Wash well. Refrigerate until ready to process.
Pretreatment: Blanch in boiling water to crack the skins.
Drying time: Dehydrator: 12 to 24 hours; sun: 1 to 2 days.
Dryness test: No sign of moisture; sticky.
Storage time: 4 to 6 months at 70 degrees F.

CURRANTS

Selection: Only ripe and firm black seedless currants should be dried. Black currants, such as the Black Corinth, are a variety of grapes and dry well. Do not dry red currants.
Preparation: Do not remove stems. Wash well.
Pretreatment: None.
Drying time: Dehydrator: 12 to 24 hours; sun: 1 to 2 days.
Dryness test: Leathery.
How to use: Substitute for raisins in baking cookies and breads.
Storage time: 6 to 8 months at 70 degrees F.

DATES

Preparation: Wipe dates clean with a damp cloth.   Do not wash.   Leave whole or cut into cubes.
Pretreatment: No pretreatment is necessary.
Drying time: Dehydrator: 4 to 6 hours;   sun: 2 to 8 days, depending on fruit and temperature.
Dryness test: Leathery, pliable,   slightly sticky.
Refreshing: Use dried without refreshing.
Storage time: 8 to 12 months at 70 degrees F.

FIGS

Preparation: In dry, warm sunny climates, it is preferable to partly dry on the tree.   Figs normally drop from the tree when 2/3 dry.   In coastal areas, pick fruit when ripe.
Pretreatment: No treatment necessary.
Drying time: Dehydrator: 12 to 20 hours; sun: 4 to 5 days.
Dryness test: Flesh pliable, slightly sticky, but not wet.
Storage time: 4 to 6 months at 70 degrees F.

GRAPES
(Muscat, Tokay, or any seedless grape)

Preparation: Leave whole. Grapes dry in less time if dipped in lye for 10 seconds. Or blanch 1/2 to 1 minute. Poke holes in grapes with a fork before drying.

Pretreatment: No treatment necessary.

Drying time: Dehydrator 12 to 20 hours (recommend only 1 or 2 trays be used because of excess moisture); sun: 3 to 5 days.

Dryness test: Raisin-like texture, no moist center.

Refreshing: Use dry, or soak in boiling water for 5 minutes before adding to recipe.

Storage time: 4 to 6 months at 70 degrees F.

NECTARINES AND PEACHES

Preparation: When sulfuring, pit and halve: if desired, remove skins. For steam and water blanching, leave whole, then pit and halve.

Pretreatment: Drop fruit as it is peeled and halved into a solution of ascorbic acid and water, using 1/2 teaspoon ascorbic acid to 1 quart of water. Drain and treat with sulfur fumes for 2 to 3 hours, or steam blanch for 8 minutes, or water-blanch for 8 minutes.

Drying time: Dehydrator: 36 to 48 hours; sun: 3 to 5 days.

Dryness test: Soft, pliable, no moist area in center when cut.

Refreshing: Soak 1 cup fruit in 2 cups hot water for 1 hour.

Storage time: 4 to 6 months at 70 degrees F.

PAPAYAS

Selection: Select ripened, smooth-skinned fruit.

Preparation: Wash well, cut in half and remove the black seeds. Peel and cut lengthwise into 3/8 inch thick slices.

Pretreatment: None.

Drying time: Dehydrator: 12 to 24 hours; sun: 1 to 2 days.

Dryness test: Leathery and pliable with no pockets of moisture.

How to use: Eat dry papaya alone or combine with other fruits.

Storage time: 4 to 6 months at 70 degrees F.

PEARS

Preparation: Cut in half and core. Peeling preferred.

Pretreatment: Drop fruit as it is, peeled and halved (or sliced), into a solution of 1 quart water and 1/2 teaspoon ascorbic acid. Drain. Treat with sulfur fumes for 5 hours or steam-blanch for 6 minutes.

Drying time: Dehydrator: 24 to 36 hours; sun: 5 to 6 days.

Dryness test: Suede-like and springy. No moisture when cut and squeezed.

Refreshing: Use dried, or cover with an equal amount of water and refrigerate overnight. To stew, simmer 1 cup dried pears with 2 cups water until tender, about 10 to 20 minutes. Sweeten after pears are tender.

Storage time: 4 to 6 months at 70 degrees F.

PERSIMMONS

Preparation: Use firm fruit when using the long, softer variety, and use riper fruit when using the round, drier variety. Peel and slice with stainless steel knife.

Pretreatment: No treatment necessary.

Drying time: Dehydrator: 18 to 24 hours; sun: 5 to 6 days.

Dryness test: Light to medium brown. Tender, but not sticky.

Storage time: 2 to 4 months at 70 degrees F.

PINEAPPLE

Preparation: Select ripe, slightly soft, fragrant pineapples. Wash the fruit, remove the spikes, and peel. Remove thorny eyes and slice, dice, or cut into 1/2 inch thick strips.
Pretreatment: None is needed.
Drying time: Dehydrator: 24 to 36 hours; sun: 3 to 4 days.
Dryness test: Firm and dry to the center.
Refreshing: Eat dried, or soak for several hours in the refrigerator.
Storage time: 6 to 8 months at 70 degrees F.

PLUMS AND PRUNES

Preparation: For sun-drying, dip in boiling lye solution or blanch in boiling water or steam for 1 to 1 1/2 minutes, to "crack" skins. For oven drying, rinse in hot tap water. Leave whole. If sulfuring, pit and halve.
Pretreatment: No treatment necessary. However, sulfuring for one hour will produce good flavor and color.
Drying time: Dehydrator: 24 to 36 hours; sun: 4 to 5 days (3 to 4 days when using lye).
Dryness test: Leathery. If whole, prune pit should not slip when squeezed.
Refreshing: Use dried, or soak overnight in water or liquid to cover. To cook, simmer in water until tender.
Storage time: 6 to 12 months at 70 degrees F.

RHUBARB

Rhubarb is a vegetable. Since it is served in desserts as a fruit it is listed here. Always discard all parts of the leaves because they are toxic.

Varieties best for drying: The bright red sweeter varieties such as Canada Red, MacDonald, Ruby, Valentine or Victoria.

Preparation: Wash, trim and slice diagonally into 1 inch slices. Discard leaves.

Pretreatment: Steam blanch for 1 to 2 minutes until slightly tender but not soft.

Drying time: Dehydrator: 12 to 24 hours; sun: 1 to 2 days.

Dryness test: Tough, no visible moisture.

How to use: Rhubarb may be used as a filling for pies, strudels, tarts or other baked goods.

Storage time: 2 to 4 months at 70 degrees F.

STRAWBERRIES

Selection: Firm, ripe, red berries with full red color.

Preparation: Gently wash,   remove the cap and cut into 1/2 inch slices, or cut smaller berries in half.   Dry skin-side down.   Berries sliced too thin will stick to the drying surface.

Pretreatment: None is needed. Dip in a solution of 1/2 teaspoon ascorbic acid to 1 cup water to increase   vitamin C content.

Drying time: Dehydrator: 12 to 24 hours; sun: 1 to 2 days.

Dryness test: Pliable, leathery, no sign of moisture.

How to use: Eat dry alone or use on cereals and ice cream.   Do not refresh strawberries because they become mushy.

Storage time: 4 to 6 months at 70 degrees F.

FRUIT LEATHERS

Leathers or roll ups, are pureed fruits and vegetables that have been dried to a chewy, leathery consistency. They may be sweet or sour in flavor.

Kids young and old alike, find the leathers to be almost an irresistible taste treat. They are like chewy nutritious candy and make popular snacks. Calorie conscious people appreciate roll ups cut into chip size pieces for use with dips.

Hikers find fruit leather to be a lightweight and satisfying food to carry on the trail. Sometimes called fruit rolls or fruit taffies, leathers can be made into a beverage by adding 5 parts of water to 1 part leather in a food blender.

Three to 4 cups of prepared fresh fruit will make two cookie sheet size leathers depending on the type of fruit and the size of the pieces. So your fruit goes a long way to make these tasty treats.

Cooks use vegetable leathers to flavor favorite pasta sauces and fruit leathers in place of raisins or candied fruit in baking. They can also be used in pie filling, or dessert topping.

These tasty rolls of pliable dried fruit may be made from virtually all fruits and berries. Any type of fruit can be used: apples, apricots, bananas, grapes, berries, pineapple, oranges, pears, peaches, tomatoes, plums, exotic fruits, etc.

Grapefruits, lemon, persimmons, and rhubarb are not usually suitable for fruit roll ups.

Leather Preparation
1. Select ripe or slightly overripe fruit.
2. Remove pits from fruit. Berry or grape seeds need not be removed. Peeling is optional, depending upon individual preference.
3. Cut fruit into chunks and place in a food chopper or blender. Juicier fruits should be blended first because their water and syrup will help the blender mix the fruit.
4. Yellow or light-colored fruit can be pretreated with 1 tablespoon of lemon or lime juice (2 tablespoons of Meyer variety lemon juice) for each quart of fruit.
5. Chop, grind, or blend to a thick puree. Water can be added to fruit to get the blender started.
6. Add 2 tablespoons of sugar per quart to sweeten orange and pineapple pulp (additional sugar is not needed for other fruits).
7. Spices can be added to fruit leather at a ratio of 1/8 teaspoon per cup.
8. Line a cookie sheet or similar flat tray with saran or waxed paper, or use your Ronco Fruit Roll-Up and Liquid Tray. Make sure that the cookie sheet or tray has an edge to prevent overflow of fruit puree.
9. Pour fruit puree onto the sheet or tray about 1/4 inch deep. Distribute evenly by tilting the

tray; do not use a spatula or knife. When all spaces are covered, the right amount of puree has been applied.

10. When leather is partially dry but still moist, chopped nuts can be sprinkled over the top.

SUN DRYING
This will take from two to three days depending upon temperature and humidity. Test frequently for dryness.

If the weather is hot (above 85 degrees F.) and dry (less than 60 percent relative humidity), the trays can be placed in direct sunlight or behind a pane of glass or plexi-glass to concentrate the heat. Cover or bring inside at night if the nighttime temperatures vary more than 20 degrees F. from daytime temperatures, or if fog or humidity is common at night.

DEHYDRATOR DRYING
Place sheets or trays in the dehydrator. Dry for 5 to 12 hours and test for dryness.

TESTING FOR DRYNESS
Properly dried fruit leather will be sticky to the touch, but will peel easily from the Ronco Fruit Roll-Up Tray or the tray lined with saran, or waxed paper. Lift the edge (which will adhere tightly to the surface) and peel it back about an inch. If it peels readily, it is properly dried.

STORAGE

After loosening the edge and peeling it back about an inch, roll the saran, or waxed paper and the dried leather in one piece in a loose roll. The dried fruit roll can be stored for years in the freezer, for months in the refrigerator, and lasts up to 6 months at room temperature.

FRUIT LEATHER RECIPES

APPLE LEATHER. Prepare about one quart chopped apples, removing cores but not skins. Place just enough water in blender, with a few apple chunks, to start the blender in action...keep adding apples until consistency is that of good applesauce. Spread apple puree evenly onto plastic or Ronco Fruit Roll-Up Trays about 1/4 inch thick. Continue with steps from leather preparation directions above.

APPLE BUTTER LEATHER. Blend 2 TB cider vinegar or lemon juice, 2 tsp mixed spices (such as pumpkin pie spice, or your own blend - coriander, nutmeg, etc.) with 1/4 cup honey. Prepare one quart chopped apples, removing cores but not skin. Add just enough water to start blender. Add apples to blender and mix until consistency of apple sauce. Continue with steps from leather preparation directions above.

APPLE-RAISIN (or DATE) ROLL UP. Soak 1 cup raisins (or chopped dates) in 1 1/2 cups water until soft and water is absorbed. Prepare about one quart chopped apples, removing cores but not skins. Place 2 cups of apples and just enough water in blender to start blender. Keep adding apples until consistency is that of good applesauce. Continue with steps from leather preparation directions above.

APPLE & FRUIT COMBO LEATHERS. Start with a one-to-one ratio for all fruits and experiment to taste. Try blending apples with dates, plums, peaches, apricots, bananas, tangerines, etc. Experiment with many combinations and proportions. You can test the concoction as you go. If you like the taste as you blend it, you will find it tasty as a leather. You may wish to blend "seedy" berries alone, then strain and return to blender before adding apples. However, seeds are an excellent, concentrated food.

SWEET FRUIT LEATHER. Prepare 1 pound each of dates, figs, raisins, and apricots and place in blender. Mix well, add water to start blender if needed. Add 1 pound shredded coconut and 2 cups chopped pecans (or other nuts, to taste). Continue with steps from leather preparation directions above.

GRAPE LEATHER. Grapes make a delicious leather. Cook the grapes 15 to 20 minutes in a double boiler to avoid scorching. Press through a sieve or food mill to remove seeds and tough skins. Add sugar to taste (1 tablespoon per cup of puree). Most grape varieties need no sweetening. Spices may be added. Continue with steps from leather preparation directions above.

PEACH LEATHER. Prepare 1 quart peeled, chopped peaches. Place peaches, 2 TB lemon juice, 3 TB of honey and 1/2 TB ground coriander in blender. Continue with steps from leather preparation directions above.

PLUM LEATHER. Prepare 1 quart peeled, chopped plums. Place plums and 1/2 TB ground cinnamon in blender. Continue with steps from leather preparation directions above.

STRAWBERRY LEATHER. Prepare 1 quart chopped strawberries. Place strawberries and 1/2 TB ground mace in blender. Continue with steps from leather preparation directions above.

SPICY LEATHER. Prepare 2 cups each of apples, apricots, and pears. Place 3 TB lemon juice, 1/2 TB Cinnamon, and 1/2 TB Nutmeg in blender. Continue with steps from leather preparation directions above.

MARBLED LEATHER. Prepare two separate batches of fruit puree using two different fruits. Tasty combinations are apple-pear, apple-peach, apricot-pineapple, cherry-raspberry, and peach-plum. Pour equal amounts of the two purees on the Ronco Fruit Roll-Up Tray or a tray lined with saran, or wax paper. Use a rubber spatula to gently swirl fruit purees together for a marbled effect.

LEATHER ROLLS WITH FILLING. Try spreading cream cheese, peanut butter, cheese whiz, nutmeat spreads, ricotta cheese or any of your favorite spreads onto the leather. Then roll the leather up and slice into small pieces to make a healthy snack or appetizer.

LEATHER FRUIT SAUCE. Fruit leather pieces can be placed in the blender and pureed to make a fruit sauce or dessert topping. Add 1 cup of water for each cup of fruit to blender and puree until smooth.

SWEET TOMATO LEATHER. Tomatoes, (especially the meaty, pear-shaped varieties) make good leather. Small cherry tomatoes or varieties with high solid content work best. Add a lemon wedge and 1 tablespoon of honey per cup of tomato puree to make the leather deliciously sweet.

TOMATO VEGETABLE LEATHER. Use 1 medium onion, 1 green pepper, and 1 garlic clove per 3 cups of prepared tomatoes. Whirl prepared onion, green pepper, and garlic in blender until fine. Add diced, unpeeled tomatoes, and blend until smooth. Add cloves or other seasonings as desired.

Tomato leather pieces can be pureed with water and seasoning to make a superb tomato sauce.

FRUIT SNACK RECIPES

BANANA CHIPS

Peel firm, ripe bananas and slice evenly 1/4 inch thick. Dip slices in pineapple juice or lemon juice, then in granulated sugar or honey. Place on dehydrator trays or plastic wrap and dry. Banana chips are sweet and chewy.

FRUIT AND SEED BARS

The ingredients in the fruit and seed bars are held together by honey and a small amount of sugar. Make a delicious and nutrition filled bar with combinations of your favorite dried fruits.

1 cup sesame seeds
1/2 cup chopped nuts (unsalted peanuts,
cashews, or almonds)
1/2 cup sunflower or pumpkin seeds
1/2 cup each packed brown sugar and honey
1/3 tsp salt
1/2 cup each of 4 different dried fruits
1/2 cup unsweetened shredded coconut
butter

Combine sesame seeds, nuts, and sunflower or pumpkin seeds. Spread in a thin layer on rimmed baking sheet. Roast at 350 degrees F. for 15 minutes or until golden brown. Shake baking sheet occasionally. Set aside.

Combine sugar, honey, salt and dried fruits in a frying pan and bring to a boil over medium heat. Boil for 2 minutes, stirring constantly. Remove from heat. Add seeds, nuts, coconut, and mix well. Fold into buttered pie dish and fill bottom evenly. Use a buttered spoon to press mixture firmly down.

Let cool at room temperature for 30 minutes. Remove from dish. Cut into bars 1 1/4 by 4 inches. Let stand until not sticky (approximately 2 to 3 hours). Wrap bars individually or together in plastic. Bars can be stored at room temperature.

DRIED FRUIT GRANOLA MIX

1/3 cup honey
1/4 cup firmly packed brown sugar
3 cups oatmeal
l cup wheat germ
1/2 cup bran
1/2 cup whole wheat flour
1/2 cup soy flour
l cup shredded coconut
1/2 cup unsalted sunflower seeds
1/2 cup sesame seeds
1/3 cup vegetable oil
1/4 cup dried grapes
1/4 cup chopped dried apple
1/4 cup chopped dried pineapple
1/4 cup chopped dried cherries
1/4 cup chopped dried bananas
1/4 cup dried blueberries

Preheat oven to 325 degrees F. In a large bowl, mix together honey, brown sugar, oatmeal, wheat germ, bran, whole wheat flour, soy flour, coconut, sunflower seeds, sesame seeds, and vegetable oil.

Add dried fruits to above mixture. (Add or substitute favorite dried fruits as desired to recipe)

Spread not more than 1 inch deep on 1 or 2 shallow baking sheets and bake for 1 hour, stirring often.

SUMMIT GRANOLA

2 1/2 cups rolled cereals (use oatmeal alone, or combine it with rolled wheat and rolled rye)
1/4 cup sunflower seeds
1/4 cup sesame seeds
3/4 cup coconut flakes or shreds
1/4 cup wheat germ
1/2 cup sliced almonds
1/8 cup date sugar or 1/4 cup brown sugar
1/2 cup water
1/3 cup honey (or more)
1/3 cup safflower (or more)
Brewer's yeast, lecithin granules and whey powder (optional)

Mix dry ingredients. Stir in water, honey, and oil. Spread in shallow pan. Bake 2 hours at 225 degrees F. Cool. Use more honey and oil for more moisture. Eat dry or mixed with milk. For additional nutrition, add brewer's yeast, lecithin, and a little whey powder prior to eating.

OLD TIME GRANOLA

6 cups quick oatmeal
3/4 cup wheat germ
1/2 cup coconut (flaked or shredded)
1/3 cup sesame or sunflower seeds
1 cup nuts (chopped walnuts or pecans, or
peanuts)
1/2 cup salad oil
1/3 cup honey
1 1/2 tsp vanilla
1 cup of your favorite chopped, dried fruit

Heat oatmeal in a shallow pan at 350 degrees F. for about 10 minutes. Combine oatmeal, wheat germ, coconut, sugar, seeds, and nuts. Add oil, honey, and vanilla. Spread on shallow pan. Bake at 350 degrees F. for 20 to 25 minutes, stirring occasionally until evenly brown. After cooling, stir until crumbles apart. Add dried fruit to cooled mixture.

SWEET PACKERS GORP

2 cups cereal (use a combination of your favorite
such as: wheat germ, oatmeal, , granola, etc.)
2 1/2 cups dried fruit (combine 3 to 4 kinds, such
as: figs, pears, apples, peaches, apricots, bananas,
dates, raisins, etc.)
3 cups nuts or seeds (combine 3 or 4 kinds, such
as: sunflower seeds, sesame seeds, coconut,
cashews, almonds, Brazil nuts, walnuts,
macadamia nuts, peanuts, pecans, etc.)
42 ounces flavored chips (combination of
semisweet chocolate chips, butterscotch chips,
and peanut butter flavored chips)
l TB honey or molasses

Assemble dry ingredients. Chop up larger pieces
of fruits and nuts. Mix dry ingredients together
in large bowl. Melt chips or morsels in top of
double boiler, stir in honey or molasses, and
pour over cereals, fruits, and nuts. Mix well, and
press or pour onto buttered cookie sheets. Cool,
and cut into 2 x 4 inch chunks. Wrap in plastic
or foil.

HIKERS ENERGY MIX

1 cup instant whole wheat cereal
1 cup quick oatmeal
2 to 3 cups chopped dates
1/2 cup dried chipped beef

Preheat oven to 400 degrees. Mix cereals and fruit and set aside. Crumble meat into fine pieces and mix with other ingredients. Store and carry mixture in a covered plastic container. Eat dry by the handful for trail food, or mix with hot water for a tasty meal.

GORP CEREAL

1 cup raw oatmeal
1/4 cup brown sugar
1 cup peanuts
1 cup raisins
Hot cocoa mix, small amount (to taste)

Mix ingredients well. Eat with milk. May be made in any amount to suit any size group.

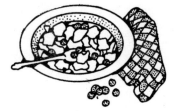

FRUIT LICORICE GORP

1 cup peanuts
1 cup raisins
1/2 cup dried papaya
1/2 cup dried pineapple
1/2 cup dried pears
1/4 cup licorice-flavored candies or gumdrops
1/4 cup small chocolate candies with varigated
color coating.

Mix ingredients well, proportions can be
changed to taste. Eat dry by the handful for trail
food.

BACKPACKERS BREAKFAST FOOD

1/4 cup natural wheat-barley prepared cereal
1/4 cup each rice cereal and oatmeal
1/4 cup high-protein prepared breakfast cereal
1/4 cup dry milk
2 tablespoons wheat germ
3 tablespoons nondairy creamer
2 tsp sugar
1/4 cup finely chopped dry fruit (dates, raisins,
prunes), or nuts (preferably cashews)

Mix all ingredients together. For cereal when
camping or hiking add water to reconstitute dry
milk and cream . For at home use, omit dry milk
and nondairy creamer and substitute with milk
for cereal.

CAROB & NUT TREAT

1/2 cup whole unblanched almonds
1/2 cup cashews
1/2 cup shredded coconut
1/2 cup dried grapes, cherries, or blueberries
1/2 cup carob chips
1/4 cup sunflower seeds
1/4 cup chopped dried apricots or peaches

Mix all ingredients together. Eat dry as a trail food.

FRUIT NUT SNACK MIX

3/4 cup dried grapes, cherries, or blueberries
1/2 cup chopped dried pears
1/2 cup chopped dried bananas
1/2 cup chopped dried apples
1/2 cup cashews
1/2 cup shredded coconut
1/2 cup whole unblanched almonds
1/4 cup chopped dried pineapple

Mix all ingredients together. Eat dry as a trail mix.

PACKERS CHOCOLATE GORP

2 cups shelled peanuts
1 cup bite-sized candy-coated chocolate bits
(such as plain M&M candies)
1 cup bite-size candy coated peanut butter bits
(such as Reese's Pieces)
1 cup whole almonds
1/2 cup chopped dried banana
1/2 cup coconut, shredded
1/2 cup apricots

Mix ingredients together. Eat dry as a trail mix.

FRUIT BREADS

APRICOT NUT BREAD

1 cup finely chopped dried apricots
1 cup warm water
1 1/3 cup all-purpose flour
2/3 cup whole wheat flour
1/4 cup dry milk
2 tsp baking powder
1 tsp salt
1/4 cup safflower oil
1 egg, beaten
1/4 cup orange juice
1 cup walnuts, chopped

Cover apricots with 1 cup warm water. Let soak 15 minutes. Drain (save 1/4 cup of the liquid). Combine oil, egg and orange juice with reserved apricot liquid. Add this mixture, the drained apricots and the walnuts, to the flour mixture. Stir just enough to moisten the dry ingredients.

Spread in greased and floured 9 x 5 inch loaf pan. Bake at 350 degrees for about 55 minutes, or until a toothpick inserted in the center comes out clean. Cool for 10 minutes. Remove from pan and finish cooling on a wire rack. Store in refrigerator until used.

BANANA BREAD

1/2 cup shortening
3/4 cup brown sugar, firmly packed
2 eggs
1 tsp grated orange peel
1 1/3 cups all-purpose flour
2/3 cup whole wheat flour
2 tsp baking powder
1/2 tsp baking soda
3/4 tsp salt
1 cup mashed banana
1/4 cup milk
3/4 cup chopped nuts
3/4 to 1 cup chopped dried apricots or dates

Preheat oven to 350 degrees F. Generously grease and flour a 9 x 5 loaf pan; set aside. In a large bowl, cream shortening with brown sugar. Add eggs and orange peel; beat well. Sift together 2 3/4 cups flour, baking powder, baking soda and salt. Add flour mixture to creamed mixture alternately with mashed banana and milk. Beat well. In a small bowl, coat nuts and chopped fruit with 1/4 cup flour. Stir into batter. Pour into prepared loaf pan. Bake in preheated oven about 1 hour, until a wooden pick inserted in the center comes out clean. Cool 10 minutes in pan. Remove from pan and cool on a cooling rack. Makes 1 loaf.

BLUEBERRY BREAD

l cup dried blueberries
4 TB butter
2/3 cup sugar
l egg
1 1/3 cups all purpose flour
2/3 cup whole wheat flour
2 tsp baking powder
l/4 tsp salt
l/2 cup milk
3/4 cup chopped nuts

Cover dried blueberries with warm water and let stand about 30 minutes to refresh.   Drain.

In a mixing bowl, cream butter and sugar until light and fluffy.   Beat in egg.   Sift together flour, baking powder, and salt.   Add flour mixture to creamed mixture alternately with milk, mixing well after each addition.   (Batter will be thick). Fold in blueberries and chopped nuts.

Pour batter into a greased 9 x 5 inch bread pan. Bake at 350 degrees F. for about 1 hour and 10 minutes, until pick inserted in center comes out clean.   Cool bread in pan.   Yield: 1 loaf.

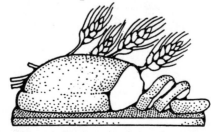

ORANGE DATE LOAF

1/4 cup butter or margarine
1/3 cup brown sugar, firmly packed
1/3 cup granulated sugar
1 egg
1 1/2 cups all-purpose flour
3/4 cup whole wheat flour
1 tsp each baking powder and baking soda
3/4 tsp salt
1 TB grated orange peel
1 cup strained fresh orange juice
1 cup chopped dates (8 oz.)
1/2 cup coarsely chopped pecans

Preheat oven to 350 degrees F. In a medium bowl, cream butter or margarine with brown sugar and granulated sugar. Add egg and beat well. Coat fruit and nuts with 1/4 cup flour. Set aside. In a medium bowl, sift together remaining flour, baking powder, baking soda and salt. In a small bowl, mix orange peel, dates and pecans with reserved 1/4 cup flour.

Alternately add sifted flour mixture and orange juice to egg mixture. Beat until blended. Stir in fruit-nut mixture. Pour into greased and floured 9 x 5 loaf pan. Bake in preheated oven in loaf pan 40 to 50 minutes or in square pan 25 to 30 minutes. Cool 5 minutes in pan. Remove from pan and cool completely on a cooling rack. Makes 1 large or 2 small loaves.

FRUIT AND BRAN MUFFINS

1 1/2 cups whole bran cereal (not bran flakes)
1/2 cup boiling water
1 egg, lightly beaten
1 cup buttermilk
1/2 cup honey
1/4 cup melted butter or margarine
1 1/2 cups mixed dried fruit (raisins, chopped
dates, prunes, or figs)
1/2 cup chopped nuts
1/2 cup whole wheat flour, unsifted
3/4 cup all-purpose flour, unsifted
1/2 tsp salt
1 1/4 tsp soda

In a large bowl, combine bran cereal with water; stir to moisten evenly, then allow to cool until lukewarm. Stir in egg, buttermilk, honey, butter, dried fruit, and nuts until well blended.

In another bowl, combine whole wheat and all-purpose flours, salt, and soda. Combine dry ingredients with liquid ingredients; stir just until evenly moistened. Spoon into greased or paper-lined muffin pans, filling them 3/4 full. Bake in a 425 degree F. oven for 20 to 25 minutes or until pick inserted in center comes out clean. Makes 12 to 16 muffins. Serve hot or cold.

BRAN MUFFINS

l cup whole-wheat flour
l/2 cup all-purpose flour
l/2 cup bran flakes
l tsp baking soda
l/4 tsp salt
l/2 to 3/4 cup dried, diced apples, apricots,
bananas, cherries, dates, prunes, pineapple or
raisins
l/3 cup chopped nuts, if desired
l egg, beaten
l l/4 cups buttermilk
l/2 cup honey
l/4 cup butter or margarine melted

Preheat oven to 350 degrees F. Grease 12 to 14 muffin pan cups; set aside. Place whole-wheat flour, all-purpose flour, and bran flakes in large bowl. Add baking soda and salt. Stir. Add dried fruit and nuts to flour mixture. Mix well to coat. In a medium bowl, mix egg, buttermilk, honey and melted butter or margarine. Pour all at once into flour and fruit mixture. Stir only until moistened. Fill muffin pan cups 3/4 full. Bake in preheated oven 20 to 25 minutes. Makes 12 to 14 muffins.

GERMAN PUFFCAKES

Boiling water
1/2 to 3/4 cup chopped dried apples, apricots,
cherries, dates, figs, pears, raisins or dried
currants
6 TB butter
6 eggs
1 cup milk
1/4 tsp salt
1 tsp sugar
1/2 tsp vanilla extract
1 cup flour
Lemon juice and powdered sugar or berry jam or
jelly, if desired

Pour boiling water over dried fruit to cover. Let stand to soften 5 to 15 minutes; drain. Preheat oven to 400 degrees F. In preheating oven, melt butter in a 13 x 9 baking pan, checking frequently to avoid scorching. In blender, combine eggs, milk, sugar and vanilla. Blend lightly to mix. Add flour. Mix well in blender. With a wooden spoon or rubber spatula, stir in chopped dried fruit. Pour into baking pan containing melted butter.

Bake 20 to 25 minutes until puffy and golden brown. If desired, sprinkle with lemon juice and powdered sugar or serve with berry jam or jelly.

FRUITY BUTTERMILK PANCAKES

Boiling water
l/2 to 3/4 cup chopped dried apples, apricots,
cherries, dates, pears or whole dried blueberries
l cup all-purpose flour
l TB sugar
l/2 tsp salt
l/2 tsp baking soda
l tsp baking powder
l egg
l l/2 cups buttermilk
3 TB vegetable oil

Pour boiling water over dried fruit to cover. Let stand to soften 5 to 15 minutes; drain. Preheat lightly oiled griddle or skillet. Sift together flour, sugar, salt, baking soda and baking powder. In a medium bowl, beat egg. Blend in buttermilk. Add flour mixture to egg mixture, mixing lightly. Stir in oil and chopped dried fruit. Batter will be slightly lumpy.

Drop batter from a large cooking spoon onto hot griddle or skillet. Turn pancakes when surface bubbles begin to break. Serve immediately. Makes eighteen to twenty 2-inch pancakes.

DESSERTS AND PASTRIES

APPLE PIE

One 9-inch pie shell
1/4 lb. dried apple slices* (3 1/2 cups)
2 cups water
1/3 to 1/2 cup sugar
1/2 tsp cinnamon

Crumb topping:
1/2 cup flour
1/4 cup brown sugar
2 1/2 TB butter or margarine

Cook dried apples in water until soft, about 1 hour. Add additional water, but not an excessive amount. Do not drain. Add sugar and cinnamon. Pour into prepared pie shell. Mix topping until crumbly and sprinkle over pie.

*Note: Either sweet or sour apples may be used in drying. Sweet apples such as Red Delicious are used for sweet schnitz (dried apples), and the peel is left on to ensure a rich flavor. If a tart flavor is preferred, use late fall or early winter fully matured apples. Varieties recommended include old favorites such as Northern Spy, Spitzenberger, Winesap, and Baldwin. Dry a small amount of a variety and test by using it in one of your favorite recipes before drying large amounts of that variety.

DRIED FRUIT CORDIALS

Dried fruit such as apricots, peaches, pears, and prunes can be immersed in white wine to give the wine a delicious light fruity taste. The wine becomes a smooth cordial that gets smoother the longer the fruit is immersed. Inexpensive wine can be used to make fruit cordials because the dried fruit mellows any harshness in the liquor.

Fruit cordials are delicious to sip, and also make a great dessert topping. After marinating in wine, the dried fruits make wonderful tasty treats.

> *1 lb dried fruit (apricots, pears, peaches or*
> *prunes with pits)*
> *1 4/5 quart bottle of dry white wine*
> *1 cup brandy*
> *2 cups sugar*

Place dried fruit in a ceramic, glass, or stainless steel container with air tight cover. Pour wine, brandy, and sugar into container and stir to blend well. Cover and let stand at room temperature for 1 week. Stir occasionally for several days until sugar is completely dissolved.

The cordial will reach peak flavor in 3 or 4 weeks. After 5 to 6 weeks, fruit may become too soft, and can be removed. Store the wine as normal.

DRIED FRUIT COMPOTE

Here is a great recipe for fruit compote. Use your favorite dried fruit such as apricots, figs, peaches, pears, pitted prunes, or raisins.

> 2/3 cup sugar (or 1/2 cup honey)
> 4 1/2 cups water
> 3 cups dried fruit
> 2/3 cup halved blanched almonds
> 1 cinnamon stick
> 3 tsp allspice
> 1/2 cup pomegranate seeds (optional)
> chopped walnuts
> whipped cream

Combine sugar and water in large pot. Over medium heat, stir until sugar is dissolved. Reduce heat to simmer gently for 5 minutes.

Cut dried fruit into small pieces and add to simmering syrup. Add almonds, nuts, cinnamon, and allspice. Cover and simmer until fruits are tender, approximately 8 to 12 minutes.

Remove from heat and let stand until lukewarm. Remove cinnamon stick. Add pomegranate seeds. Place into individual serving dishes. Chill before serving. Top with walnuts and whipped cream and serve. Serves 6.

APPLE COFFEE CAKE

2 cups dried apples
1 tsp lemon juice
1/2 cup margarine
3/4 cup sugar
2 eggs
1 1/2 cups flour
1/4 tsp salt
2 tsp baking powder
1/2 cup milk
1 tsp vanilla

Topping:
1/2 cup sugar
2 tsp cinnamon

Place apples and lemon juice in a bowl. Add enough water to cover and soak 1 hour. Cream margarine and sugar. Add eggs and beat well.

Sift together flour, salt, and baking powder. Add to creamed mixture. Add milk and vanilla. Beat well. Pour into two 9-inch greased and floured cake pans. Top with drained, rehydrated apple slices. Combine sugar and cinnamon. Sprinkle evenly over apples. Bake at 375 degrees F. for 35 to 40 minutes.

CINNAMON CRUMBLE COFFEECAKE

l/4 cup butter or margarine
l/4 cup brown sugar, firmly packed
l/4 cup granulated sugar
l egg
l tsp vanilla extract
l cup all-purpose flour
l tsp baking powder
l/4 tsp baking soda
l/8 tsp salt
l/2 cup dairy sour cream
l cup chopped dried apples, apricots, dates,
prunes or sweet cherries

Nut Topping:
l/3 cup light brown sugar, firmly packed
2 TB all-purpose flour
3/4 tsp cinnamon
3 TB butter or margarine
l/3 cup chopped nuts

Grease and flour an 8 inch square baking pan; set aside. Preheat oven to 350 degrees F. Prepare nut topping; set aside. In a medium bowl, cream butter or margarine with brown sugar and granulated sugar. Stir in egg and vanilla. Sift together flour, baking powder, baking soda and salt. Alternately add flour mixture and sour cream to egg mixture. Spread batter in bottom of prepared pan. Sprinkle chopped dried fruit over batter. Sprinkle nut topping over dried fruit. Bake in preheated oven

25 to 30 minutes. Cool 10 to 15 minutes in pan. Makes 6 servings.

Nut Topping:
In a small bowl, combine brown sugar, flour, cinnamon, and butter or margarine. Blend well with pastry blender or 2 knives. Stir in nuts.

GOLDEN FRUIT BALLS

1/2 cup each dried apricots, apples, peaches
1/2 cup finely grated unsweetened coconut
1/4 cup blanched almonds
1 tsp grated lemon peel
1/2 tsp cinnamon
3 TB honey
3 TB orange juice
1 TB lemon juice
powdered sugar, if desired

Grind apricots, apples and peaches in meat grinder or blender until pieces are the size of rock salt or finer (about 1/8 inch in diameter). Place in medium bowl. Stir in coconut, almonds, lemon peel and cinnamon. In a small saucepan, slightly warm honey, orange juice and lemon juice. Stir to mix well. Slowly pour honey mixture over fruit mixture, stirring until mixture sticks together evenly. Form into small balls about 3/4 inch in diameter. Place on baking sheets. Dry at 120 degrees F. until no longer sticky to touch, up to 6 hours on a dry day. If desired, roll balls in powdered sugar. Makes 48 golden crunchy balls.

PEAR FRITTERS

3/4 cup chopped dried pears
1 TB lemon juice
2 egg yolks, beaten
1/4 cup milk
1/3 cup dairy sour cream or nonfat yogurt
1/2 tsp vanilla extract
1 1/3 cups all-purpose flour (or 1 cup all purpose flour and 1/3 cup whole wheat flour)
2 tsp baking powder
1/2 tsp salt
1/2 tsp nutmeg
1/4 tsp cinnamon
2 egg whites
2 TB sugar
oil or shortening for frying
cinnamon sugar (see below) or powdered sugar, if desired

Toss dried pears with lemon juice and set aside. Blend egg yolks, milk, sour cream and vanilla in a large bowl. In medium bowl, sift together flour, baking powder, salt, nutmeg and cinnamon. In another medium bowl, beat egg whites until frothy. Gradually add sugar and continue beating until stiff peaks form. Add flour mixture to egg yolk mixture and blend. Fold stiffly beaten egg whites and dried pears tossed with lemon juice into batter. In a heavy pan or deep fryer, heat 2 inches of oil or shortening to 375 degrees F. Drop batter by slightly rounded teaspoonfuls into hot oil or shortening. Larger fritters will be doughy in the

center.   Fry until crisp and golden brown,
turning ounce.   Drain on paper towels.   If
desired, place in a paper bag and shake with
cinnamon sugar or powdered sugar.   Makes 35 to
40 small fritters.

Variations:
Substitute other dried fruit such as apples,
apricots, bananas, cherries, dates, peaches,
pineapple or prunes for pears.

HOT CROSS BUNS

l cup milk
3 TB butter or margarine
l/3 cup sugar
l pkg. active dry yeast
l/4 cup warm water (ll0 F.)
3/4 tsp salt
3/4 tsp cinnamon
l/2 teaspoon nutmeg
l/4 tsp ground cloves
3 l/2 to 4 cups all-purpose flour
2 eggs, beaten
3/4 cup dried currants
l/4 cup finely diced candied orange peel, citron
or pineapple
l TB oil
l egg yolk diluted with l teaspoon water
Lemon Glaze, see below

In a small saucepan, scald milk by heating until bubbles form around the edges. Add butter or margarine and sugar. Stir until sugar is dissolved. Cool to lukewarm, about ll0 degrees F. In a large bowl, dissolve yeast in warm water. Stir in lukewarm milk mixture, salt, cinnamon, nutmeg, and cloves. Stir in 2 cups flour and beaten eggs. Beat until smooth. In a small bowl, mix currants and candied fruit with 1/2 cup flour. Stir into milk mixture. Gradually add enough flour to make a stiff dough. Turn out onto a floured surface and knead until smooth and elastic, about 10 minutes. Add 1 tablespoon oil. Place dough in bowl, turning once to oil top.

Cover with a cloth. Set in a warm place free from drafts and let rise until doubled in bulk, about 1 1/2 hours. Punch down in bowl. Shape dough into 1 1/2 inch balls and place on a baking sheet. Cut a cross in top of each ball with a sharp knife or scissors. Cross should be no more than 1/8 inch deep. Brush lightly with diluted egg yolk. Cover and let rise in a warm place until doubled in bulk, 30 to 45 minutes. Preheat oven to 400 degrees F. Bake about 10 minutes or until lightly browned. Cool slightly on cooling racks. Prepare Lemon Glaze and pour into crosses on buns. Makes 30 to 35 buns.

Lemon Glaze:

Combine 1 cup powdered sugar, 1/2 tsp grated lemon peel and 1 TB lemon juice in a small bowl. Mix until smooth.

PINEAPPLE DOUGHNUTS

1 1/2 cups buttermilk
1 pkg. active dry yeast
1/4 cup sugar
1/2 cup riced cooked potatoes
2 eggs
3/4 tsp salt
1 tsp cinnamon
1/3 cup butter or margarine, melted
1 tsp grated lemon peel
1 medium apple, peeled and shredded
2 cups all-purpose flour
1 1/4 cup whole wheat flour
1 1/2 cups chopped dried pineapple
oil or shortening for frying
Cinnamon Sugar

In a small saucepan, warm buttermilk to 105 to 115 degrees F. Pour into a warmed large bowl and sprinkle with yeast. Add sugar and stir until dissolved and let stand 5 to 10 minutes. Add potatoes, eggs, salt, cinnamon, melted butter or margarine, lemon peel and apple and mix well. Add 1 1/4 cups flour. Beat until smooth and elastic. Gradually stir in remaining 2 cups flour.

Beat until very smooth. Fold in pineapple. Batter will be sticky. Cover and let rise in a warm place 1 hour or until doubled in bulk. In a heavy pan or deep fryer heat 3 inches of oil or shortening to 375 degrees F. Drop batter by heaping tablespoonsful into hot oil or shortening.

To make flat doughnuts, let batter slide off
spoon, pushing slightly with a second spoon. If
batter is dropped by rounded spoonfuls,
doughnuts may be doughy in center. Fry until
golden brown, turning once. Remove from oil.
Drain on paper towels. Shake in paper bag with
Cinnamon Sugar. Serve immediately. Makes 36
to 48 doughnuts.

CHAPTER 3

WONDERFUL
VEGETABLES

HOME DRYING VEGETABLES

Vegetables are an essential part of our meal planning, and have a variety of uses as a side dish, or in soups, salads, stews, and casseroles. Having dried vegetables conveniently available any time during the year affords us virtually unlimited use of vegetable recipes. In this chapter, each vegetable is listed with preparation and pretreatment methods, approximate drying times, how to test for dryness, and how to refresh or reconstitute. The times listed for storage are quite conservative. Vegetables can be stored for considerably longer periods of time than those mentioned. They will not spoil as long as they are properly packaged. You can drastically increase the shelf life with cooler storage or by vacuum packing.

Dried vegetables can be enjoyed by themselves for snacks or appetizers, or be refreshed and used in your favorite recipes. Have fun experimenting with the many uses of your wonderfully dried and refreshed vegetables. Individual vegetables are arranged in alphabetical order for easy reference.

HOW TO PREPARE, DRY AND REFRESH VEGETABLES

ARTICHOKE

Preparation: Cut hearts into 1/8 inch strips.
Pretreatment: Blanch in boiling solution (3/4 cup water, 1 TB lemon juice).
Drying time: Dehydrator: 12 to 16 hours; sun: 10 to 12 hours.
Dryness test: Brittle.
Storage time: 1 to 2 months at 70 degrees F.; 2 to 4 months at 60 degrees F.

ASPARAGUS

Preparation: Wash well.   Halve stalks or slice into small pieces.
Pretreatment: Water-blanch: 2 to 4 minutes; steam-blanch: 3 to 5 minutes.
Drying time: Dehydrator: 5 to 10 hours; sun 8 to 10 hours.
Dryness test: Brittle.
Refreshing: Soak in water, 2 1/4 cups water to 1 cup asparagus for 1 1/2 hours or until tender. Cook same as if fresh.
Storage time: 1 to 2 months at 70 degrees F.; 2 to 4 months at 60 degrees F.

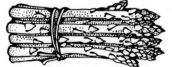

BEANS
(GREEN or WAX)

Preparation: Wash. Cut ends off and remove strings. Slice into 1/2 inch pieces or french style.
Pretreatment: Water-blanch: 2 minutes; steam-blanch: 2 1/2 minutes.
Drying time: Dehydrator: 8 to 14 hours; sun: 8 to 10 hours.
Dryness test: Brittle.
Refreshing: Soak in water, 2 cups water to 1 cup beans for 1 hour or until tender. Cook same as if fresh.
Storage time: 3 to 4 months at 70 degrees F.; 4 to 6 months at 60 degrees F.

BEETS

Selection: Use only small tender beets.
Preparation: Cut into strips 1/8 inch thick.
Pretreatment: Water blanch: 1 1/2 to 2 minutes, steam blanch: 2 to 3 minutes.
Drying time: Dehydrator: 12 to 16 hours; sun: 8 to 10 hours.
Dryness test: Tough, brittle, dark red.
Storage time: 3 to 4 months at 70 degrees F.; 4 to 6 months at 60 degrees F.

BROCCOLI

Preparation: Trim and cut stalks lengthwise, slice into small pieces 1/4 inch thick.
Pretreatment: Water-blanch: 2 minutes; steam-blanch: 3 minutes.
Drying time: Dehydrator: 10 to 16 hours; sun: 8 to 10 hours.
Dryness test: Brittle.
Refreshing: Soak in water, 2 cups water to 1 cup broccoli for 1 1/2 hours or until tender. Cook same as if fresh.
Storage time: Less than 1 month at 70 degrees F.; 1 to 2 months at 60 degrees F.

BRUSSELS SPROUTS

Selection: Use small, fresh brussels sprouts.
Preparation: Cut in half lengthwise through stem.
Pretreatment: Blanch with steam 6 to 7 minutes or in water 4 1/2 to 5 1/2 minutes.
Drying time: Dehydrator: 12 to 15 hours; sun: 8 to 12 hours.
Dryness test: Tough to brittle.
Storage time: Less than 1 month at 70 degrees F.; 1 to 2 months at 60 degrees F.

CABBAGE

Preparation: Remove outer leaves, wash, quarter, and core. Cut into strips 1/8 inch thick.
Pretreatment: Water-blanch: 1 1/2 to 2 minutes; steam-blanch: 2 1/2 to 3 minutes or until wilted.
Drying time: Dehydrator: 10 to 11 hours; sun: 6 to 8 hours.
Dryness test: Leather to brittle.
Refreshing: Soak in water, 3 cups water to 1 cup cabbage for 1 hour or until tender. Cook same as if fresh.
Storage time: Less than 1 month at 70 degrees F.; 1 to 2 months at 60 degrees F.

CARROTS

Preparation: Wash, cut off roots and tops, peeling is optional. Slice into strips 1/8 inch thick.
Pretreatment: Water-blanch: 3 to 5 minutes; steam blanch: 4 to 6 minutes.
Drying time: Dehydrator: 10 to 12 hours; sun: 8 to 10 hours.
Dryness test: Tough to brittle.
Refreshing: Soak in water, 2 1/4 cups water to 1 cup carrots for 1 hour or until tender. Cook same as if fresh.
Storage time: 4 to 6 months at 70 degrees F.; 6 to 8 months at 60 degrees F.

CAULIFLOWER

Preparation: Wash flowerets and remove from core, splitting stems so flowerets are not more than 1 inch thick.
Pretreatment: Blanch with steam for 4 to 5 minutes or in water for 3 to 4 minutes.
Drying time: Dehydrator: 12 to 15 hours; sun: 8 to 10 hours.
Dryness test: Tough to brittle.
Storage time: Less than one month at 70 degrees F.; 1 to 2 months at 60 degrees F.

CELERY

Preparation: Trim, wash stalks and leaves well. Cut leaves from stalks. Thinly slice stalks. Leaves will dry faster so remove from dryer as they dry.
Pretreatment: Water blanch: 2 to 3 minutes, or steam blanch: 3 to 4 minutes.
Drying time: Dehydrator: 12 to 15 hours; sun: 8 to 10 hours.
Dryness test: Brittle.
Refreshing: Soak in water, 2 cups water to 1 cup celery for 1 hour or until tender. Dry celery leaves can be used for seasoning.
Storage time: 1 to 2 months at 70 degrees F.; 2 to 4 months at 60 degrees F.

CORN

Preparation: Select fresh corn with milky kernels. Husk, remove silks, blemishes, and trim.

Pretreatment: **Corn on the cob**: Blanch in boiling water for 2 to 2 1/2 minutes. Steam blanch for 3 to 4 minutes until the milk does not exude from the kernels.

Corn, cut: Cut the corn from the cob with a sharp knife after blanching.

Drying time: Dehydrator: 6 to 10 hours; sun: 6 to 8 hours.

Dryness test: Brittle, very dry.

Refreshing: Soak in water, 2 1/4 cups water to 1 cup corn for 1/2 hour or until tender. Cook same as if fresh.

Storage time: 3 to 4 months at 70 degrees F.; 6 to 8 months at 60 degrees F.

CUCUMBERS

Preparation: Peel and cut into slices 1/8 inch to 1/4 inch thick.

Pretreatment: None needed.   Salting is optional, sprinkle with small amount of salt to aid drying and to season the chips.

Drying time: Dehydrator: 10 to 12 hours; sun 6 to 8 hours.

Dryness test: Leathery to crisp.

Refreshing: Eat dry alone or as a chip with dip.

Storage time: 1 to 2 months at 70 degrees F.; 2 to 4 months at 60 degrees F.

EGGPLANT

Preparation: Wash, peel, trim and slice firm eggplant into 1/4 inch slices.

Pretreatment: Dip prepared slices into salt water solution of 1 teaspoon salt to 1 quart of water. Water-blanch: 1 1/2 minutes; steam-blanch: 2 1/2 to 3 minutes.

Drying time: Dehydrator: 10 to 16 hours; sun: 6 to 8 hours.

Dryness test: Leathery, dry, brittle.

Refreshing: Soak in water, 2 cups to 1 cup eggplant for 1 1/2 hours or until tender.   Cook same as if fresh.

Storage time: 1 to 2 months at 70 degrees F.; 2 to 4 months at 60 degrees F.

GARLIC

Preparation: Use firm garlic with no bruises. Separate into cloves and peel outer skin.   Slice in half lengthwise.
Pretreatment: None needed.
Drying time: Dehydrator: 8 to 12 hours; sun: 8 to 10 hours.
Dryness test: Crisp, very brittle.
How to use: Garlic salt can be made using a blender to chop garlic into powder.   Combine 4 parts salt for each part of garlic and blend for just two seconds.
Storage time: 2 to 4 months at 70 degrees F.; 4 to 6 months at 60 degrees F.

HORSERADISH

Preparation: Wash; remove all small root pieces   and stubs.   Peel or scrape roots.   Grate. No blanching needed.
Pretreatment: None needed.
Drying time: Dehydrator: 12 to 16 hours; sun: 6 to 8 hours.
Dryness test: Very dry and powdery.
Storage time: 2 to 4 months at 70 degrees F.; 4 to 6 months at 60 degrees F.

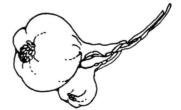

KOHLRABI

Selection: The thick base of the stem is edible and can be dried. Use stems 2 to 3 inches in diameter.
Preparation: Wash, trim root ends and the vine-like stems. Peel thinly and slice 1/8 to 1/4-inch thick.
Pretreatment: Water blanch: 4 to 5 minutes or steam blanch: 5 to 8 minutes.
Drying time: Dehydrator: 10 to 16 hours; sun: 6 to 8 hours.
Dryness test: Leathery to brittle.
Storage time: 1 to 2 months at 70 degrees F.; 2 to 4 months at 60 degrees F.

MUSHROOMS

Preparation: Wash well. Discard any tough stalks. Slice into sections 1/8 to 1/4 inch thick. Small mushrooms can be dried whole.
Pretreatment: None needed. Mushrooms can be kept from darkening by dipping slices into a solution of 2 tablespoons vinegar to 1 quart of water, or a solution of 1/2 teaspoon ascorbic acid to 1 quart of water.
Drying time: Dehydrator: 8 to 10 hours; sun: 6 to 8 hours.
Refreshing: Can be added to soups and sauces without refreshing.
Storage time: 1 to 2 months at 70 degrees F.; 2 to 4 months at 60 degrees F.

OKRA

Preparation: Wash, trim, and slice crosswise in 1/4 to 1/8 inch strips. Blanch with steam for 4 to 5 minutes or in water 3 to 4 minutes.
Drying time: Dehydrator: 8 to 12 hours; sun: 6 to 10 hours.
Test for dryness: Tough to brittle.
Refreshing: Soak in water, 3 cups water to 1 cup okra for 3/4 hour or until tender. Cook same as if fresh.
Storage time: 2 to 4 months at 70 degrees F.; 4 to 6 months at 60 degrees F.

ONIONS

Preparation: Wash, remove outer "paper shells", cut off roots and tops. Cut into slices 1/8 to 1/4 inch thick.
Pretreatment: None needed.
Drying time: Dehydrator: 10 to 20 hours; sun: 8 to 11 hours.
Dryness test: Leathery to brittle.
Refreshing: Soak in water, 2 cups water to 1 cup onions for 3/4 hour or until tender. Use same as if fresh.
Storage time: 2 to 4 months at 70 degrees F.; 4 to 6 months at 60 degrees F.

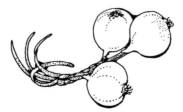

PARSLEY

Preparation: Wash well. Trim and discard coarse stems. Leave leaves in small clusters.
Pretreatment: None needed.
Drying time: Dehydrator: 1 to 2 hours; sun: 6 to 8 hours.
Dryness test: Brittle and flaky.
Refreshing: Use dry as seasoning. Parsley does not reconstitute well.
Storage time: 3 to 4 months at 70 degrees F.; 4 to 6 months at 60 degrees F.

PEAS

Selection: Use only sweet young tender varieties.
Preparation: Wash, shell.
Pretreatment: Water blanch: 2 to 3 minutes; steam blanch: 3 to 4 minutes.
Drying time: Dehydrator: 8 to 10 hours; sun: 6 to 8 hours.
Refreshing: Soak in water, 2 cups water to 1 cup peas for 1 1/2 hours or until tender. Cook same as if fresh.
Storage time: 6 to 8 months at 70 degrees F.; 8 to 12 months at 60 degrees F.

PEPPERS AND PIMIENTOS

Preparation: Wash, stem, and remove seeds and partitions. Slice into disks 1/8 to 1/4 inch thick.

Pretreatment: None needed.

Drying time: Dehydrator: 8 to 12 hours; sun: 6 to 8 hours

Dryness test: Leathery to brittle.

Refreshing: Soak in water, 2 cups water to 1 cup vegetable for 1 hour or until tender.

Storage time: 6 to 8 months at 70 degrees F.; 8 to 12 months at 60 degrees F.

POPCORN

Preparation: Harvest ears of corn when ripe and hang until well dried. Remove kernels and place on dehydrator trays or in the sun to fully dehydrate.

Pretreatment: None needed.

Drying time: Dehydrator: 8 to 12 hours; sun: 10 to 12 hours.

Dryness test: Shriveled, very dry.

How to use: Use same as store bought popping corn.

Storage time: 4 to 6 months at 70 degrees F.; 8 to 10 months at 60 degrees F.

POTATOES

Selection: Russett,   Burbank,   and   White   Rose.
Preparation: Wash   and   peel.   Cut   into
shoestring   strips   1/4   inch   thick,   or   cut   in   slices
1/8   inch   thick.
Pretreatment: Water   blanch: 4   to   5   minutes,
or   steam   blanch: 6   to   8   minutes.
Drying time: Dehydrator: 8   to   12   hours;   sun: 6
to   8   hours.
Refreshing: Soak   in   water,   2 1/2   cups   water
to   1   cup   potatoes   for   1 1/2   hours   or   until   tender.
Cook   same   as   if   fresh.
Storage time: 2   to   4   months   at   70   degrees   F.;
4   to   6   months   at   60   degrees   F.

PUMPKIN

Preparation: Wash   rind   and   dry.   cut   in   halves,
remove   seeds   and   scrape   pulp.   Cut   into   1   inch
wide   strips   about   1/8   inch   thick.
Pretreatment: Water   blanch: 1 1/2   to   2
minutes,   steam   blanch: 2   to   3   minutes.
Drying time: Dehydrator: 10   to   16   hours;   sun:
6   to   8   hours.
Refreshing: Soak   in   water,   3   cups   water   to   1
cup   pumpkin   for   1   hour   or   until   tender.
Storage time: Less   than   1   month   at   70   degrees
F.;   1   to   2   months   at   60   degrees   F.

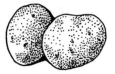

RUTABAGAS

Preparation: Wash, thinly peel, and cut into slices 1/4 to 1/2 inch thick.
Pretreatment: Water blanch: 3 to 4 minutes or steam blanch: 4 to 5 minutes.
Drying times: Dehydrator:12 to 16 hours; sun: 6 to 8 hours.
Dryness test: Leathery to brittle.
Refreshing: Use in soups and stews without refreshing.
Storage time: 1 to 2 months at 70 degrees F.; 2 to 4 months at 60 degrees F.

SPINACH AND OTHER GREENS

Selection: Use tender young leaves.
Preparation: Wash, trim stems.
Pretreatment: Water blanch: 1 to 2 minutes, Steam blanch: 2 to 3 minutes.
Drying time: Dehydrator: 6 to 10 hours; sun: 8 to 10 hours.
Dryness test: Brittle.
Refreshing: Soak in water, 1 cup water to 1 cup greens for 1/2 hour or until tender.
Storage time: 1 to 2 months at 70 degrees F.; 2 to 4 months at 60 degrees F.

<u>SQUASH</u>

Preparation: **Banana**:   Wash, peel, and cut
into strips 1/4 inch thick.
Hubbard: Wash rind and dry.   Cut in halves,
remove seeds, and scrape pulp.   Cut   into 1 inch
wide strips, peel off rind.   After peeling cut
strips about 1/8 inch thick.
Summer and Zucchini: Wash, trim, and slice
into strips 1/4-inch thick.   For large squash, peel
and remove seeds.
Pretreatment: Water-blanch: 1 to 1 1/2
minutes; steam-blanch: 2 1/2 to 3 minutes.
Drying time: Dehydrator: 10 to 16 hours; sun:
6 to 8 hours.
Dryness test: Leathery to brittle.
Refreshing: Soak in water, 1 3/4 cups water
to 1 cup squash for 1 hour or until tender.   Cook
same as if fresh.
Storage time: Less than 1 month at 70
degrees F.; 1 to 2 months at 60 degrees F.

SWEET POTATOES OR YAMS

Preparation: Wash and peel.   Cut into strips 1/4 inch thick.

Pretreatment: Water blanch: 1 1/2 to 2 minutes, or steam blanch: 2 to 3 minutes or until almost tender.

Drying time: Dehydrator: 10 to 16 hours; sun: 6 to 8 hours.

Dryness test: Leathery to brittle.

Refreshing: Soak in water, 1 1/2 cups water to 1 cup sweet potatoes for 1/2 hour or until tender.   Cook same as if fresh.

Storage time: Less than 1 month at 70 degrees F.; 1 to 2 months at 60 degrees F.

TOMATOES

Selection: Firm ripe tomatoes with good color.

Preparation: Slice into sections about 1/4 inch thick.   Small pear or plum tomatoes can be simply cut in half.

Pretreatment: Water blanch 1 to 2 minutes, or steam blanch: 2 to 3 minutes.

Drying time: Dehydrator: 10 to 24 hours; sun: 8 to 16 hours.

Dryness test: Leathery to brittle.

Refreshing: Soak in water, 2 cups water to 1 cup tomatoes for 1 1/2 hours or until tender.

Storage time: 2 to 3 months at 70 degrees F.; 3 to 4 months at 60 degrees F.

TURNIPS

Preparation: Wash, remove tops and thinly peel. Cut into slices 1/4 inch thick.
Pretreatment: Water blanch: 4 to 5 minutes, or steam blanch: 6 to 8 minutes.
Drying time: Dehydrator: 10 to 16 hours; sun 6 to 8 hours.
Drying test: Leathery to brittle.
Refreshing: Soak in water, 1 cup water to 1 cup turnips for 3/4 hour or until tender. Cook same as if fresh.
Storage time: 1 to 2 months at 70 degrees F.; 2 to 4 months at 60 degrees F.

ZUCCHINI CHIPS

Preparation: Cut into slices 1/4 to 1/8 inch thick. Peeling is optional.
Pretreatment: None is needed. Salting is optional, sprinkle small amount of salt to aid drying and to season the chips.
Drying time: Dehydrator: 10 to 12 hours; sun: 6 to 8 hours.
Dryness test: Crisp and brittle.
Refreshing: Eat dry alone or as a chip with dip.
Storage time: Less than 1 month at 70 degrees F.; 1 to 2 months at 60 degrees F.

SOUP & VEGETABLE RECIPES

VEGETABLE SOUP MIX

*(Take this soup mix along for picnics,
camping, or hiking)*

2 tsp instant chicken-flavored bouillon
l/4 cup dried carrot slices
l/4 cup dried celery slices
l/4 cup dried diced green pepper
l/8 tsp dried thyme

Combine all ingredients in small food container
until ready to use.

To prepare soup, stir mixture into 2 cups boiling
water.   Reduce heat, cover pot, and simmer 15 to
20 minutes.   Yield: Two 1-cup servings.

VEGETABLE SOUP

4 cups water
3/4 to 1 cup dried vegetables
(green beans, corn, peas, tomatoes, onions, etc.)
2 pkg. beef bouillon granules or 4 cubes
Season to taste

Bring water to a boil.   Add dried vegetables, bouillon, and seasonings.   Simmer about 20 minutes or until vegetables are tender though chewy.

For variety, add 1/2 cup rice, noodles, or barley with the other ingredients, or add 1/4 to 1/2 cup dried jerky, cut in bite-size pieces.

Using low-sodium soup granules or bouillon cubes will allow those on low-sodium diets to enjoy this versatile recipe.

BEEF VEGETABLE SOUP

1 meaty soup bone
1 cup ass't dried vegetables (corn, peas, beans)
1 large stalk celery, diced
2 carrots, diced
1 medium onion, diced
1 TB dried parsley
1 TB salt
1/4 tsp pepper

Place soup bone in large saucepan and add water to cover. Bring to boil. Reduce heat and simmer 1 hour.

Pour boiling water over dried vegetables just to cover. Soak 1 hour.

Add diced vegetables, dried parsley, and seasonings, to the beef bone. Add the dried vegetables in their water to above mixture. Simmer 1 to 1 1/2 hours.

Remove bone, dice meat, and return to pot. Season to taste and serve hot.

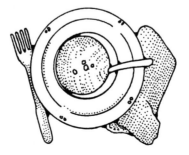

INSTANT SOUP CUP

1 TB dried vegetable powder (such as peas)
1/4 cup dried milk
6 oz. boiling water

Pulverize dried vegetables into powder in a blender or food processor at the highest speed.

Mix powder with dried milk. Place in cup and add boiling water. Stir. For better flavor, soup may be simmered. Dried potato flakes may be added, if desired, to thicken soup.

CREAMED CORN

1 1/2 cups dried corn kernels
3 cups boiling water
3/4 cup half-and-half (light cream)
1 tsp sugar
1/4 cup butter or margarine
salt and ground black pepper

Refresh dried corn in a medium saucepan by covering with boiling water. Let stand 2 hours.

Add half-and-half, sugar, butter, salt and pepper to taste. Cover and simmer for 1 hour or until corn is soft. Watch carefully so that corn does not boil dry and burn. Yield: 4 to 6 servings.

CORN CHOWDER

1/2 cup dried corn
1 1/2 cups water
4 strips bacon
1 medium onion, chopped
2 cups water
1 medium potato, diced
2 1/2 cups water
2 cups nonfat dry milk
1 TB flour
1 1/2 tsp salt
1/8 tsp pepper

Refresh corn in 1 1/2 cups of water. Allow to stand for at least 30 minutes. Brown bacon in soup pot until crisp. Remove and drain. Brown onion in bacon fat until tender. Add onion to bacon. Discard all fat except for 2 tablespoons.

Place undrained refreshed corn into soup pot. Add 2 more cups of water. Boil for 45 minutes. If necessary, add more water to maintain volume. Add diced potato and cook until tender. Combine premeasured milk, flour, salt, and pepper mixture with 2 1/2 cups water and mix well. Add milk mixture to the pot and bring to a simmer, stirring occasionally. Add onions and crumbled bacon. Stir well. Serve with crackers or homemade bread. Backpackers: Save trouble by mixing dry milk, flour, salt, and pepper before leaving home.

CORN FRITTERS

1 cup dried corn
4 cups boiling water
1 1/2 cups flour
1 tsp baking powder
1 tsp salt
2 eggs, beaten
1/2 cup milk

Refresh corn by adding to boiling water and allow to stand for 20 minutes.

Simmer corn until tender, approximately 1 hour. Drain off excess water (save for soup or gravy).

Sift flour, baking powder, and salt into a bowl.

Combine the beaten eggs and milk, mixing well.

Add the liquid to the flour mixture all at once and stir the mixture until smooth. Fold in the corn.

Drop batter from a teaspoon into a well-greased frying pan and cook until brown on all sides.

Remove and drain on absorbent paper. Serve hot.

WINTER CORN PUDDING

3/4 cup dried corn
3 cups boiling water
2 eggs, slightly beaten
2 TB butter, melted and slightly cooled
2 cups light cream
2 TB onion, chopped
1 TB sugar
1 tsp salt
1/8 tsp pepper

Refresh corn by adding to boiling water and allow to stand for 20 minutes.

Simmer corn until tender, approximately 1 hour. Drain excess water (save for soup or gravy).

Preheat the oven to 325 degrees F. and grease 1 quart casserole.

In a large bowl, combine corn, eggs, melted butter, light cream, onion, sugar, salt, and pepper.

Pour into the greased casserole and bake for 35 minutes or until knife inserted in the center comes out clean.

<u>GREEN BEAN CASSEROLE</u>

2 cups water
1 cup cut green beans, dried
1 can mushroom soup
1/4 tsp onion powder

Bring water to a boil. Add beans and cook to desired degree of firmness.

Add can of soup and onion powder. Simmer in saucepan until heated through and serve.

Variation--Place in 1 quart casserole. Top with bread crumbs or french fried onion rings. Bake in 325 degree F. oven for 30 to 35 minutes.

PLUMANTE

(Can be used as an edible garnish, served as an appetizer, tossed in salads, vegetables or pasta.)

Plumante (Italian dried tomatoes in oil) can be easily made for a fraction of what it costs in specialty food shops. When preparing this recipe use the best quality olive oil and the smallest tomatoes you can find.

3 pounds Roma or small pear-shaped tomatoes
salt
2 or 3 cloves garlic, peeled
2 or 3 small sprigs rosemary
olive oil

Slice tomatoes lengthwise almost in half. Lay them open like a book (cut side up) on dehydrator or other drying trays. Sprinkle cut surfaces lightly with salt

Dry in either a dehydrator or oven at 120 degrees F. to 140 degrees F. for about 4 hours. It may take longer in a dehydrator. When tomatoes are dry, they will have shriveled to small, flattish ovals and will feel dry but still pliable. They should not be brittle.

Place tomatoes, garlic, and rosemary loosely into 2 or 3 half-pint jars. Pour in enough oil to cover tomatoes completely. Cap jars. Let stand in a cool, dark place for 1 month for flavors to develop. The dried tomatoes keep at room temperature for as long as the oil remains fresh.

CHAPTER 4

MEMORABLE
JERKY

DRYING MEATS

Jerky has become an increasingly popular snack. Interest in making home dried jerky has risen sharply because it's easy to make, easy to carry, and most of all a great tasting snack. Beef is the most common type of jerky made. Jerky can also be made from fish, poultry and other meats.

Below are step by step instructions for making jerky with memorable good flavor. Meats, fish, and poultry should be handled with care and always prepared in a timely manner.

Caution is especially important when pretreating and storing raw meat for the process of making jerky. If not properly prepared, meat can easily spoil or become contaminated.

Before preparing game meat for drying, it should be frozen at zero degrees for at least two months. This will destroy harmful micro-organisms in the meat.

Raw poultry and pork should not be used to make jerky because of the danger of trichinosis disease.

Lean meat is recommended for making jerky. During drying, fat becomes rancid and slows

down the drying process.   Cut away as much fat
as possible from the meat before drying.

Marinades with salt or soy sauce are used to
break down the meat tissues and prepare it for
drying.   Liquid smoke, which flavors food with a
smoke taste, can be purchased at the grocery
store.   Liquid smoke used in small amounts
makes a tasty addition to marinade recipes.

Marinating of meats should always be done in
the refrigerator.   Raw meat should never be left
on the kitchen counter or at room temperature
to marinate. Meats should also be thawed in the
refrigerator as well.

Jerky must be dried at a constant temperature
between 140 to 150 degrees F. for four hours to
protect it from spoiling.   After drying for four
hours the temperature can be lowered to 130
degrees F. for slower drying and a higher quality
jerky.

After marinating, the meat should be cut into
pieces that are uniform in size. It's
recommended that you use a very sharp knife.
Try partially freezing the meat to make it easy
to slice thinly.   To make a more tender jerky,
cut across the grain of the meat.

The slices should be about 5 inches long by 1
1/2 inch wide and 1/8 to 1/4 inch thick.   Spread
the sliced meat evenly on dehydrator trays. The
pieces should not be overlapped. Filling 3/4 of

the surface area of the trays is a good rule of thumb.

As the meat drys, oil may appear. Remove the oil by patting with a paper towel. Allow the meat to dry until its texture is dry enough that it will crack when you bend it, but not brittle enough to crack in two.

Test the meat often as it drys to avoid over drying. Fish and turkey require less drying time than beef.

Finished jerky can be kept in the refrigerator to preserve its flavor longer. Generally, jerky will keep for about two months.

Here's a special word about salt. All salt contains sodium, and sodium has been found to increase the risk of heart related problems. Eat dried jerky meat in moderation because it contains a high amount of sodium from salt and soy sauce.

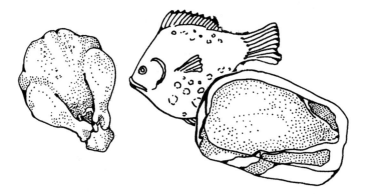

BEEF JERKY RECIPES

The following beef jerky recipes can also be used for making jerky with veal, lamb, turkey, venison, and other game meats.

RANCH STYLE JERKY
Makes about 1/2 lb jerky

1 tsp pepper
1/2 cup soy sauce
1-2 cloves garlic, crushed
2 TB cider vinegar
1 tsp snipped chives
2 lbs. round, flank steak, or other lean cut meat

Mix marinade ingredients together in a bowl. Dip meat slices into marinade. Place dipped meat in layers in a bowl or dish. Pour remaining marinade sauce over meat. Cover tightly and let marinate in refrigerator for 6 to 12 hours. Rotate layers of meat occasionally.

Place in dehydrator until dry. While meat is drying, blot excess oil with paper towel.

GINGER JERKY
Makes about 1/2 lb jerky

1/2 tsp salt
1/2 tsp pepper
1/2 tsp ground ginger
1 TB fresh ginger
1 large clove garlic, minced
1/2 cup soy sauce
1/4 cup firmly packed brown sugar
2 lbs round, flank steak, or other lean cut meat

Mix marinade ingredients together in a bowl. Dip meat slices into marinade. Place dipped meat in layers in a bowl or dish. Pour remaining marinade sauce over meat. Cover tightly and let marinate in refrigerator for 6 to 12 hours. Rotate layers of meat occasionally.

Place in dehydrator until dry. While meat is drying, blot excess oil with paper towel.

TAILGATER'S JERKY
Makes about 1/2 lb jerky

1 tsp salt
1/4 tsp pepper
1/8 tsp cayenne pepper
1 tsp onion powder
1/8 tsp ground cloves
1/2 tsp garlic powder
1 tsp dry mustard
3 TB brown sugar
1/3 cup cider vinegar
1/3 cup barbecue sauce
2 lbs round, flank steak or other lean cut meat

Mix marinade ingredients together in a bowl. Dip meat slices into marinade. Place dipped meat in layers in a bowl or dish. Pour remaining marinade sauce over meat. Cover tightly and let marinate in refrigerator for 6 to 12 hours. Rotate layers of meat occasionally.

Place in dehydrator until dry. While meat is drying, blot excess oil with paper towel.

ARIZONA STYLE JERKY
Makes about 1/2 lb jerky

2 tsp salt
1 tsp pepper
1 tsp ginger
1/4- 1/2 tsp cayenne pepper
3 TB chili powder
2 tsp cumin
2 cloves garlic, minced
2 TB fresh cilantro, minced
2 lbs round, flank steak, or other lean cut meat

Mix all ingredients together. Place meat slices side by side on a flat surface. Sprinkle marinade mix on meat, turn meat and sprinkle the other side. Rub mix into meat. Place in a covered non-metal dish and let marinate in refrigerator for 6 to 12 hours.

Place in dehydrator until dry. While meat is drying, blot excess oil with paper towel.

TERIYAKI JERKY
Makes about 1/2 lb jerky

1/2 cup teriyaki sauce
1/4 tsp salt
1/4 tsp pepper
1/2 tsp ground ginger
2 TB brown sugar
1 garlic clove, crushed
2 lbs round, flank steak, or other lean cut meat

Mix marinade ingredients together in a bowl. Dip meat slices into marinade. Place dipped meat in layers in a bowl or dish. Pour remaining marinade sauce over meat. Cover tightly and let marinate in refrigerator for 6 to 12 hours. Rotate layers of meat occasionally.

Place in dehydrator until dry. While meat is drying, blot excess oil with paper towel.

SMOKED HAMBURGER JERKY
Makes about 1/2 lb jerky

1/2 cup soy sauce
1 TB allspice
4 TB sugar
2 tsp fresh grated ginger
1 clove garlic, minced
1 TB liquid smoke
2 lbs hamburger, leanest grade possible

Press hamburger meat into flat strips 5 inches long by 1 1/2 wide and 1/4 inch thick. Place one layer of hamburger strips in dish for marinating.

Mix marinade ingredients together in a bowl. After well mixed , sprinkle marinade sauce over meat, soaking well. Turn meat over and sprinkle with sauce. Add layers of hamburger strips to marinating dish and repeat sprinkling of marinade. Pour remaining marinade sauce over meat. Cover tightly and let marinate in refrigerator for 6 to 12 hours. Rotate layers of meat occasionally.

Place in dehydrator until dry. While meat is drying, blot excess oil with paper towel.

<u>WESTERN JERKY</u>
Makes about 1/2 lb jerky

4 tsp salt
1 tsp each pepper, chili powder, garlic powder,
and onion powder
1/4 tsp cayenne pepper
3 dashes liquid smoke
1 half cup water
2 lbs round, flank steak, or other lean cut meat

Mix marinade ingredients together in a bowl. Dip meat slices into marinade. Place dipped meat in layers in a bowl or dish. Pour remaining marinade sauce over meat. Cover tightly and let marinate in refrigerator for 6 to 12 hours. Rotate layers of meat occasionally.

Place in dehydrator until dry. While meat is drying, blot excess oil with paper towel.

STEPHAN'S CALIFORNIA JERKY
Makes about 3/4 lb jerky

1/2 cup soy sauce
1/4 cup Worcestershire sauce
1/3 cup lemon juice
1/4 cup oil and vinegar dressing
1 tsp pepper
1/2 tsp salt
3 - 4 cloves garlic, crushed
1 TB liquid smoke
mixture of your favorite herbs
3 lbs round, flank steak, or other lean cut meat

Mix marinade ingredients together in a bowl. Dip meat slices into marinade. Place dipped meat in layers in a bowl or dish. Pour remaining marinade sauce over meat. Cover tightly and let marinate in refrigerator for 6 to 12 hours. Rotate layers of meat occasionally.

Place in dehydrator until dry. While meat is drying, blot excess oil with paper towel.

MOUNTAIN HIGH JERKY
Makes about 1/2 lb jerky

1 tsp salt
1 tsp pepper
3 TB brown sugar
1/4 cup Worcestershire sauce
1/4 cup Tamari sauce
1/8 tsp snipped chives
1 tsp liquid smoke
2 lbs round, flank steak, or other lean cut meat

Mix marinade ingredients together in a bowl. Dip meat slices into marinade. Place dipped meat in layers in a bowl or dish. Pour remaining marinade sauce over meat. Cover tightly and let marinate in refrigerator for 6 to 12 hours. Rotate layers of meat occasionally.

Place in dehydrator until dry. While meat is drying, blot excess oil with paper towel.

CURRY SPICED JERKY
Makes about 1/4 lb jerky

1 tsp salt
1/4 tsp pepper
1/2 tsp cinnamon
1/8 tsp ground cloves
1/8 tsp ground cumin
1 1/2 tsp curry powder
1/2 tsp garlic powder
1 tsp ground ginger
1 lb round, flank steak, or other lean cut meat

Mix all ingredients together. Place meat slices side by side on a flat surface. Sprinkle marinade mix on meat, turn meat and sprinkle the other side. Rub mix into meat. Place in a covered non-metal dish and let marinate in refrigerator for 6 to 12 hours.

Place in dehydrator until dry. While meat is drying, blot excess oil with paper towel.

<u>CURRY JERKY</u>
Makes   about   1/2   lb   jerky

1   tsp   salt
1/4   tsp   pepper
1   tsp   allspice
1/8   tsp   ground   nutmeg
1/2   tsp   ground   cumin
1   TB   curry   powder
1   tsp   ground   ginger
1-2   cloves   garlic,   minced
2   lbs   round,   flank   steak,   or   other   lean   meat

Mix all ingredients together. Place meat slices side by side on a flat surface. Sprinkle marinade mix on meat, turn meat and sprinkle the other side. Rub mix into meat. Place in a covered non-metal dish and let marinate in refrigerator for 6 to 12 hours.

Place in dehydrator until dry. While meat is drying, blot excess oil with paper towel.

DUDE RANCH JERKY
Makes about 1/4 lb jerky

1/4 cup pineapple juice
1/4 cup soy sauce
1 tsp salt
1 tsp ground ginger
1 TB brown sugar
1/4 tsp pepper
1/8 tsp cayenne pepper
1 garlic clove, crushed
1 lb round, flank steak, or other lean cut meat

Mix marinade ingredients together in a bowl. Dip meat slices into marinade. Place dipped meat in layers in a bowl or dish. Pour remaining marinade sauce over meat. Cover tightly and let marinate in refrigerator for 6 to 12 hours. Rotate layers of meat occasionally.

Place in dehydrator until dry. While meat is drying, blot excess oil with paper towel.

JERKY OLE'
Makes about 1/4 lb jerky

1 tsp salt
1/4 tsp pepper
1/4 tsp ground cumin
1/2 tsp garlic powder
1/2 tsp oregano, crushed
1 tsp paprika
1 tsp chili powder
1 lb round, flank steak, or other lean   cut meat

Mix all ingredients together.   Place meat slices
side by side on a flat surface.   Sprinkle marinade
mix on meat, turn meat and sprinkle the other
side.   Rub mix into meat.   Place in a covered non-
metal   dish and let marinate in refrigerator for 6
to 12 hours.

Place in dehydrator until dry.   While meat is
drying, blot excess oil with paper towel.

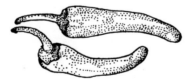

SESAME SEED JERKY
Makes about 1/4 lb jerky

1/2 cup soy sauce
1/2 tsp salt
1/4 tsp pepper
2 tsp sugar
1 TB red wine
2 TB sesame seeds
1 lb round, flank steak, or other lean cut meat

Mix marinade ingredients together in a bowl. Dip meat slices into marinade. Place dipped meat in layers in a bowl or dish. Pour remaining marinade sauce over meat. Cover tightly and let marinate in refrigerator for 6 to 12 hours. Rotate layers of meat occasionally.

Place in dehydrator until dry. While meat is drying, blot excess oil with paper towel.

SWEET SOUR JERKY
Makes about 1/4 lb   jerky

1 tsp salt
1/4 tsp pepper
1/2 tsp onion powder
1 garlic clove, crushed
2 TB brown sugar
2 TB sweet sour sauce
1/4 cup red wine vinegar
1/4 cup pineapple juice
1 lb round, flank steak, or other lean   cut meat

Mix marinade ingredients together in a bowl. Dip meat slices into marinade. Place dipped meat in layers in a bowl or dish. Pour remaining marinade sauce over meat. Cover tightly and let marinate in refrigerator for 6 to 12 hours. Rotate layers of meat occasionally.

Place in dehydrator until dry. While meat is drying, blot excess oil with paper towel.

LOUISE'S HOT JERKY
Makes about 1/2 lb jerky

1 cup water
1/3 cup soy sauce
1 TB red wine or dry sherry
1/4 cup brown sugar
1 tsp salt
1/2 tsp cinnamon
3/4 tsp anise seed
5 thin slices of fresh ginger
1 tsp onion powder
1/8 tsp ground cloves
1/8 tsp cayenne pepper
3 small dried hot chili peppers, minced
2 lbs round, flank steak ,or other   lean   cut meat

Mix marinade ingredients together in a bowl. Dip meat slices into marinade.   Place dipped meat in layers in a bowl or dish.   Pour remaining marinade sauce over meat.   Cover tightly and let marinate in refrigerator for 6 to 12 hours. Rotate layers of meat occasionally.

Place in dehydrator until dry.   While meat is drying, blot excess oil with paper towel.

SMOKED TURKEY JERKY
Makes about 1/2 lb jerky

1/2 cup soy sauce
4 TB sugar
2 tsp fresh grated ginger
1 clove garlic, minced
1 TB liquid smoke
2 lbs cooked turkey sliced paper thin. (Turkey thighs   or breasts are best)

Mix marinade ingredients together in a bowl. Dip meat slices into marinade. Place dipped meat in layers in a bowl or dish. Pour remaining marinade sauce over meat. Cover tightly and let marinate in refrigerator for 6 to 12 hours. Rotate layers of meat occasionally.

Place in dehydrator until dry. While meat is drying, blot excess oil with paper towel.

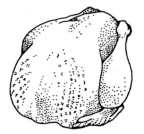

BRIAN'S HOT GAK JERKY
Makes about 1/4 lb jerky

1/4 cup water
1 TB salt
1 tsp pepper
1 tsp onion powder
1 tsp lemon juice
1 tsp Worcestershire sauce
2 small dried hot chili peppers
12 drops Tabasco sauce
1/4 tsp thyme
1 lb round, flank steak, or other lean cut meat

Mix marinade ingredients together in a bowl. Dip meat slices into marinade. Place dipped meat in layers in a bowl or dish. Pour remaining marinade sauce over meat. Cover tightly and let marinate in refrigerator for 6 to 12 hours. Rotate layers of meat occasionally.

Place in dehydrator until dry. While meat is drying, blot excess oil with paper towel.

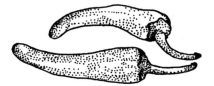

PEMMICAN MIXES

SPICED PEMMICAN

1/2 cup each apricots, dates and raisins
1/2 cup dried beef
Peel of 1 orange, grated
3/4 cup firmly packed brown sugar
1 tsp cinnamon
1/2 tsp each nutmeg, and allspice
Pinch salt
1 tsp vanilla
1 TB each vinegar, oil, and maple syrup
1/2 of a beaten egg
1/2 cup flour
Cider, brandy, or rum to make a heavy dough.

Mix chopped dried fruits, dried beef, and orange peel thoroughly with spices, sugar, flavoring, vinegar, oil, syrup, egg, and flour. Work in enough cider, brandy or rum to make a heavy dough. Put dough into an 8 inch pan and bake at 325 degrees F. for an hour or longer, until it sets well and is not too sticky. Spiced Pemmican can be kept for several weeks.

FRUIT-NUT PEMMICAN

2 cups mixed nuts
1 1/2 cups raisins
8 ounces dried dates
8 ounces dried beef or jerky
Honey to make stiff dough
Salt to taste

Grind up nuts, raisins, dates, and meat. Mix thoroughly in large bowl. Stir in enough honey to give the mixture the consistency of stiff dough. Add salt if needed. Pack in plastic bags.

DRIED FRUIT PEMMICAN BARS

Dried fruits, desired kinds and quantities to taste
Nuts, kinds and quantities to taste
Powdered sugar

Put the dried fruits and nuts through a coarse meat grinder. Spread the mixture out on a cookie sheet and cut into bars. Cover loosely and let stand for about 2 weeks, until rather dried out. Dust with powdered sugar. Wrap bars individually in foil, and refrigerate.

MINCEMEAT RECIPES

When making mincemeat there is a lot of room to experiment with a variety of ingredients. Mincemeat is made from several basic ingredients that must be included in any recipe, and from a wide range of optional ingredients.

Unique and personal recipes can be made by experimenting with different mixes and measures of ingredients.

These basic ingredients must be included in mincemeat; meat, suet, fruit juice or broth, raisins, apples, spices, currants, and citron.

Optional ingredients for mincemeat are far ranging and limited only by creativity. Dried fruits in varieties of combinations and measures are regularly used. Peaches, pears, dates, and apricots make outstanding additions to mincemeat.

Canned fruit can be added to give the mincemeat a slightly different flavor than dried fruit. Canned pineapple, peaches, pears, and cherries are popular in recipes.

Fresh lemon and orange peel, as well as candied fruit peels, are tasty additions to mincemeat pies. Fresh fruit juices can be included in mixtures to help sweeten or tart the flavor.

Some recipes call for vinegar or the juices from pickled fruits to give the mincemeat a sharp taste. A cup of coffee is often used to flavor and darken the mincemeat.

Either sugar or syrup can be used for the basic sweetening. You can use any type. Raw, white, brown, and maple sugar all work well. Maple syrup, molasses, corn syrup, sorghum and honey can all be used for sweetening.

Fruit juice or broth is used to keep the mincemeat moist and prevent it from drying out while it is cooking. Sweet cider is the most commonly used juice. Alternatives are orange juice, grape juice, or the syrup from canned fruits.

Different liqueurs can be added to the mincemeat after it has finished cooking. Choose from brandy, rum, hard cider, liqueur, and wine to suit your mood and taste.

Nuts are also added to the mincemeat after it has cooked to enhance the flavor. Mix in any combination of your favorites.

Experimenting with mincemeat and the various ingredients is fun, however be careful not to go overboard. Sometimes more is not better, and too many optional ingredients will muddle the taste.

To store the mincemeat, place it into a container with a lid that is air tight. For each gallon of mincemeat, pour one pint of wine or liquor over the mincemeat to help preserve it.   Mincemeat will keep for several weeks in the refrigerator.

Pieces of cooked meat, fruits, and liquids can be added to the mincemeat at any time while it is stored.   All the ingredients to be added must be fresh, the meat fully cooked, and the fruits and vegetables boiled.   Be sure all ingredients are cool before adding them to the mincemeat.

Mincemeat can be frozen by placing it into freezer containers leaving a 1/2 inch head space to allow for expansion during freezing.   Freeze the mincemeat at zero degrees F. or below. Ideally it should be frozen at minus 10 degrees F.

The   mincemeat recipes on the following pages have recommended ingredients and proportions. You can experiment and change the ingredients or proportions to suit your taste or available ingredients.

DELIGHTFUL MINCEMEAT

4 cups lean ground beef or ground venison
8 cups peeled chopped apples
2 cups beef suet
2 cups raisins
2 cups currants
1 cup chopped citron
4 cups sugar and corn syrup (mix 2 cups each)
4 cups dried fruit
4 cups broth or fruit juice
1 tsp each of cinnamon, cloves, nutmeg
1 tsp salt

Mix all ingredients together and transfer to a kettle. Simmer mixture for at least an hour, stirring often. Remove from heat when the mincemeat is thickened and the apples are tender. When a spoonful of mincemeat is placed on a dish, liquid should not separate from it.

Add fruit juice to the mincemeat if it becomes dry before it is fully cooked. After the mincemeat is cooked and cooled, you may add nuts, marmalade, jam, or brandied fruits. Try one to two cups of one or more of them.

After the mincemeat is finished, two cups of liqueur or wine can be poured over it to help preserve it and enhance the flavor. Cover the mincemeat and let it ripen in the refrigerator for three weeks.

VENISON MINCEMEAT

5 cups lean ground venison
1 cup ground beef suet
10 cups tart apples peeled and chopped
4 cups seedless raisins
2 cups dried apricots
1 cup currants
1 cup chopped citron
1 tsp each of cloves, cinnamon, allspice
1 tsp salt
3 cups brown sugar
2 cups honey
1 quart sweet cider

Mix ingredients in a large kettle and simmer for at least one hour. Stir constantly and add more sweet cider if the mincemeat becomes dry while cooking.

SWEET PEAR MINCEMEAT

12 medium sized pears, peeled
1 orange unpeeled
1 lemon unpeeled
2 cups dried peaches
2 cups raisins
2 cups sugar or corn syrup
1/2 tsp each of nutmeg, mace, cinnamon
1/4 cup crystallized ginger, chopped
1/4 cup grand marnier
4 drops angostura bitters

Cut up orange and lemon to remove seeds. Use the coarse blades of a food processor to grind pears, orange, and lemon together. Add raisins, sugar, spices, and ginger to the fruit. Mix in a kettle and bring to a boil. Stir constantly as it comes to a boil.

Reduce heat and cook for about 30 minutes. Remove from heat when the mincemeat has thickened and appears glossy. Stir in the grand marnier and the drops of angostura bitters.

TOMATO MINCEMEAT

4 cups unripe tomatoes
1 orange unpeeled
1/2 cup tart apples peeled
1/4 cup chopped beef suet
1/2 cup dried apricots
1/2 cup maple sugar
1/4 cup apple cider
1/2 tsp cinnamon
1/4 tsp each of nutmeg and ginger
1 tsp salt

Chop tomatoes with course blade, sprinkle with
salt and let stand for one hour.   Add 8 cups
boiling water to tomatoes and let stand for 5
minutes. Drain water from tomatoes. Cut orange
into quarter slices to remove seeds.   Chop orange
and add it along with   the rest of the ingredients
to the tomatoes.   Simmer for about an hour,
while stirring, until mincemeat is thickened.

DRIED FRUIT MINCEMEAT

2 cups beef tongue
4 cups dried apples
1 cup dried peaches
1/2 cup each prunes and apricots
1/2 cup each raisins and currants
1/2 cup amaretto liqueur
4 cups light brown sugar
4 cups sweet cider
2 cups pineapple juice
1 cup almond slices
1 cup mix of orange and lemon peels, chopped
1/2 candied pineapple
1 tsp mace
1 cup orange marmalade

Cut the fruits into small thin slices. Mix all the fruits in a bowl with amaretto liqueur and let marinate over night.

Cook beef tongue until tender. Trim outer layer and discard. Chop tongue in food processor using medium blade. Mix tongue with dried fruits, currants, brown sugar, sweet cider, and pineapple juice. Simmer, while stirring, until thickened and fruits are tender.

Before removing from heat, stir in candied pineapple, orange and lemon peels, and mace. Remove from heat and mix in the marmalade and almonds. After finished mixing, pour the liqueur over the mincemeat.

DRIED FISH

Dried fish can be made from any type of lean fish with white meat.   Lean fish is used for the same reasons as lean beef, to avoid the risk of fat becoming rancid during the drying process.

Cod is the most popular fish used for drying because it is lean and has a very appealing flavor. Any firm fish such as red snapper or sea bass will work well. Swordfish, salmon and tuna are also excellent. Whatever type of fish used, it must be the freshest possible.

Only fresh fish should be dried.   Store bought fish should not be used for drying unless it can be determined that it is indeed fresh.

Since fish spoils quickly, it must be prepared and dried immediately after bringing it home.   After cleaning and filleting the fish,   cut it into 5 inch long strips by 1 inch wide and 1/4 inch thick.

For very small fish, it is not necessary to cut them into pieces, they can be dried whole. After the fish is properly sized, it must be marinated in a salt brine before it can be dried.

The salt brine will remove much of the moisture from the fish. Start by soaking the fish with a salt rinse which is made by stirring one cup of pickling salt into a gallon of water.

Soak the fish in the salt water for several minutes. Then place the fish where the water can drain. After excess water has drained, rub salt into the pieces of fish.

Use 1/2 pound of pickling salt for each two pounds of fish. Fine grain pickling salt should be used for rubbing into the fish. The fine grains work into the fish more readily.

After rubbing salt into the fish, the pieces are ready to be placed in a curing container. Lay the fish with the skin side down in the container. The fish pieces may be layered over one another.

It is best to use a container that will allow the excess moisture to drain from the fish. A wooden tray with holes on the bottom, or wooden lath type tray placed in a container works well to keep the fish above any juices that pool at the bottom of the container.

Place the container in the refrigerator to cure for 4 to 6 hours. After the fish has finished curing, the fish must be rinsed. Mix equal parts of vinegar with water to wash away as much of the salt as possible.

The fish is now ready to marinate. Dip each fish into a bowl of marinating sauce so it is well soaked. (Use marinating recipes that follow). Place fish into marinating dish that has an air tight cover. Pour the remaining marinating sauce over the fish and allow to soak in sauce.

Cover marinating dish and place in refrigerator to marinate for 6 to 12 hours. The amount of marinating time depends on how thick the fish pieces are, and the number of layers.

As with meat, the fish should be dried at a constant 140 to 150 degrees F. The dried fish will feel dry and firm when finished - although it should not be hard or brittle. If you press your finger on it, the fish meat should depress and rise back again.

Dried fish will keep for about two months if kept in air and moisture proof containers.

FISH JERKY RECIPES

SMOKED SALMON JERKY
Makes about 1/2 lb jerky

1/2 cup soy sauce
2 tsp liquid smoke
2 lbs salmon, boned and skinned

Pretreat and cure fish according to earlier directions.

Mix marinade ingredients together in a bowl. Dip fish slices into marinade. Place dipped fish slices in layers in a bowl or dish. Pour remaining marinade sauce over fish. Cover tightly and let marinate in refrigerator for 6 to 12 hours. Rotate layers of fish occasionally.

Place in dehydrator until dry. While fish is drying, blot excess oil with paper towel.

SALMON JERKY
Makes about 1/2 lb jerky

1/4 cup soy sauce
2 TB water
2 TB brown sugar
1 TB grated fresh ginger
2 lbs salmon, boned and skinned

Pretreat and cure fish according to earlier directions.

Mix marinade ingredients together in a bowl. Dip fish slices into marinade. Place dipped fish slices in layers in a bowl or dish. Pour remaining marinade sauce over fish. Cover tightly and let marinate in refrigerator for 6 to 12 hours. Rotate layers of fish occasionally.

Place in dehydrator until dry. While fish is drying, blot excess oil with paper towel.

JERRY'S JERKY SPECIAL
Makes about 1/2 lb jerky

1/2 cup teriyaki sauce
2 TB parsley flakes
1/2 TB cracked pepper
1/2 tsp celery salt
1/2 bay leaf, crushed
2 TB dry sherry
2 lbs sea bass, sword fish, cod, or salmon, boned
and skinned

Pretreat and cure fish according to earlier directions.

Mix marinade ingredients together in a bowl. Dip fish slices into marinade. Place dipped fish slices in layers in a bowl or dish. Pour remaining marinade sauce over fish. Cover tightly and let marinate in refrigerator for 6 to 12 hours. Rotate layers of fish occasionally.

Place in dehydrator until dry. While fish is drying, blot excess oil with paper towel.

LONG JON TUNA JERKY
Makes about 1/2 lb jerky

1/2 cup soy sauce
4 TB sugar
2 tsp grated fresh ginger
1 clove garlic, minced
2 lbs fresh raw tuna, boned and skinned cut into
1/4 inch thick strips

Pretreat and cure fish according to earlier
directions.

Mix marinade ingredients together in a bowl.
Dip fish slices into marinade. Place dipped fish
slices in layers in a bowl or dish. Pour remaining
marinade sauce over fish. Cover tightly and let
marinate in refrigerator for 6 to 12 hours.
Rotate layers of fish occasionally.

Place in dehydrator until dry. While fish is
drying, blot excess oil with paper towel.

SWEET AND SOUR FISH
Makes about 1/2 lb jerky

2 tsp honey
1 TB water
2 TB soy sauce
2 TB dry sherry or rice wine
1 TB vegetable oil
juice of 1/2 lemon
2 lbs sea bass, sword fish, cod, or salmon, boned
and skinned

Pretreat and cure fish according to earlier directions.

Mix marinade ingredients together in a bowl. Dip fish slices into marinade. Place dipped fish slices in layers in a bowl or dish. Pour remaining marinade sauce over fish. Cover tightly and let marinate in refrigerator for 6 to 12 hours. Rotate layers of fish occasionally.

Place in dehydrator until dry. While fish is drying, blot excess oil with paper towel.

HOT STUFF FISH JERKY
Makes about 1/2 lb jerky

1/2 cup soy sauce
2 cups brown sugar
2 TB ground pepper
1 1/2 TB cayenne pepper
1 TB garlic powder
1 TB onion powder
2 lbs sea bass, sword fish, cod, or salmon, boned and skinned

Pretreat and cure fish according to earlier directions.

Mix marinade ingredients together in a bowl. Dip fish slices into marinade. Place dipped fish slices in layers in a bowl or dish. Pour remaining marinade sauce over fish. Cover tightly and let marinate in refrigerator for 6 to 12 hours. Rotate layers of fish occasionally.

Place in dehydrator until dry. While fish is drying, blot excess oil with paper towel.

CHAPTER 5

HERBS, POTPOURRI, AND DRY FLOWERS

Drying is a great way to enjoy your garden herbs and flowers long after the growing season has ended. Dried herbs and flowers, if harvested and processed correctly, will retain much of their appearance and fragrance.

Both flowers and herbs should be harvested just prior to full bloom. This is when the aroma is at its peak.

Collect the herbs and flowers on a dry day after the morning dew has dissipated and before the hot sun has a chance to remove the flowers' scent. Harvest only small amounts that can be worked with at once. You'll get better results if you are not trying to process too much material.

DRYING HERBS

Harvest herbs just as they begin to bloom, for peak flavor. Herbs should be cut with a six inch length of stem if possible, so they can be tied in bunches. After collecting herbs, rinse in cold water, if needed, to remove dust and dirt. If the leaves are free of dirt and dust, rinsing is not recommended. Shake off excess water and place herbs on towels to drain away moisture.

Herbs are easily dried in a dehydrator. Your Ronco Herb Screen will help keep the herbs from falling through the tray. Dehydrator drying is especially good for preserving the colors and oils in herbs.   Ideal drying temperature is 110 degrees F.

Place the herbs on the Ronco Herb Screen without overlapping them. The herb screen is placed over the dehydrator trays. If you're not using your Ronco Herb Screen place the herbs on trays for drying.   It is easier to dry small leaf herbs with the stems and leaves intact. After drying, the leaves can easily be stripped from the stems. Large leaves of herbs like basil or comfrey can be pulled from stems before they are placed on trays.

The secret of drying herbs is to draw the moisture out of them quickly in order to preserve the oils that give the herbs their color and flavor.

The herbs are dry when the stems become brittle and the leaves crumble easily. A good test for dryness is to place a tablespoon of the herbs in a tightly sealed glass jar and watch for condensation, mold or discoloration to develop. Your herbs are not sufficiently dehydrated if it does. Basil is an herb you must watch carefully for moisture retention. Once you're sure your herbs are sufficiently dehydrated, remove the leaves from the stems and store in air tight containers in a cool, dry, and dark place.

Light and heat will not only fade the color of the herbs but also erode their flavor. It is best to store herbs in glass containers. Paper or cardboard containers should not be used because they absorb the herb oils and take the flavor away.

Save the dried herb stems as an aromatic for burning in the fireplace, or burn in the barbeque to flavor grilled food.

Storing dried herbs is simple, takes up little space, and is convenient. Herbs can be stored in jars near the kitchen stove so they can easily be added to recipes as needed.

Dried herbs do not have the same taste as fresh herbs, but they have flavor qualities that are so valuable to recipes.

There are other ways to preserve herbs. They can be preserved in butter and used in virtually an unlimited number of ways. Chopped herbs can be frozen in ice cubes and added to soups, juices, sauces, stews, or stuffing.

AIR DRYING HERBS

Tie the herbs into small bunches with string or twine. Hang the bunches in a place where the air is hot, dust free, and dark. The attic is a good place to hang and leave the herbs to dry.

Another very popular method is to place bunches of herbs in a brown paper bag. Place the herbs with the leaves facing downward with the stems protruding out the open end of the bag. Tie the open end of the bag around the stems with string and hang in a hot, dark area. The paper bag keeps dust and light away from the herbs.

DRYING HERB SEEDS
Most herb seeds should be harvested after the seed pods have changed color and before they crack open. Place the herb seed pods on drying trays.

The seeds will easily fall from the pods when they are dry by rubbing them in your hands. The seeds should be kept whole until they are to be used. Herb seeds keep for several years if left whole.

HERB TEA BLENDS
Use your fresh and dried herbs to make your own blends of herb teas. Here are combinations of herbs that blend well together to make flavorful teas. Have fun experimenting with these combinations of blends, or your own to discover new flavors.

- blueberry, camomile, and spearmint
- blackberry leaves and orange peel
- cinnamon, sage, and nutmeg
- camomile, rosemary, and borage
- camomile, hops, and valerian
- camomile and peppermint
- orange peel and spearmint
- orange peel, cinnamon, and clove

•hibiscus, lemon grass, and alfalfa
•orange peel and chicory
•rose hips, ginger, and orange peel
•rosemary, lemon peel, and cinnamon
•strawberry leaf and almond extract
•cardamom and nettle
•fennel and dandelion root
•peppermint, spearmint, and lemon peel
•lemon grass and clove
•lemon balm, lavender, and rosemary
•pineapple, sage, and ginger
•thyme, bergamot, and ginger
•wood betony and orange peel

DRYING FLOWERS

As with harvesting herbs, flowers should be collected on dry days after the dew has evaporated. Collect only the best flowers for drying because when dried the imperfections become magnified.

Its a good idea to collect more flowers than you will actually need. Give yourself extra material to work with and allow for damages and plants that do not dry properly.

Air drying of flowers is the same as drying herbs. They are tied into a bunch and left to hang upside down in a hot, dust free, dark room with air circulation. Using the Ronco Food Dehydrator will dry them naturally in about 1/2 the time or less. Select petals from the flower and place them loosely on the dehydrator trays. It will take approximately 5 hours to dry the flowers depending upon how many trays you're using.

Flowers that are dried quickly will have the highest quality of texture and color. It is best to dry flowers immediately after harvesting. Tie the plants into small bunches of no more than 10 to 20 stems and keep the flowers of the same length together. The flower heads should not be pressed together because they will be distorted.

Hang the flowers upside down from hooks or rods. Lattice and racks also work well as does chicken wire suspended from the ceiling.

Hanging the flowers upside down will give them a straight natural look when dry. However, some flowers are more appealing if they are allowed to dry with the stems down. As you dry flowers experiment to find which flowers are more attractive if dried with stems down. A wire screen that allows the stems to pass through the screen works well to hold flowers upright.

Hanging plants with stems up or down has an advantage of making flowers dry straight. Although if all the plants in an arrangement are straight, the arrangement appears too stiff.

It is a good idea to dry some of the plants differently. Dry some of the flowers on paper sheets. Place them flat on the paper and allow to bend naturally as they dry. Turn the flowers every few days to keep free of mildew.

Some plants can be dried standing up in containers and will develop natural postures as they dry. By drying flowers in different ways you will get interesting and highly attractive arrangements.

NATURAL EVAPORATION
Natural evaporation is an alternative method to air drying. This technique allows flowers to dry

slowly while standing in a container. Place the flowers stem down in a container filled with one to two inches of water. Let plants stand until dry. This method usually produces more natural appearing dried flowers.

There are some flowers that are too delicate to stand up by themselves after drying. The heads of these flowers tend to droop or hang awkwardly. These flowers need to be supported with wire to make them suitable for dry arrangements.

Buy six or eight inch lengths of florist wire, usually 21 gauge works best, and wire the flowers before drying.

To wire flowers, begin by cutting the stems 1/2 inch from the flower head. Insert the wire through the stem and into the flower. The wire should be pushed through just enough to enter the flower head. It should not be pushed so far that it sticks out of the flower.

The wire will be snugly held in place as the flower and stem dries around it. False stems can be purchased and added to cover the lower part of the wire to finish the flowers.

DRYING WITH SAND
While the air drying technique is used most of the time, there are needs for more sophisticated drying results. Another method of drying to

make dried flowers appear life like is to use fine sand.

Sand drying of flowers is a very old form of drying. It began centuries ago. This method uses very fine sand to surround the flower petals while moisture evaporates from them. The sand must be very clean, free of dust, silt, and salt.

Place the flowers to be dried in containers and fill in the sand around them until they are completely covered. Lids are not placed on the containers so the air can circulate and the moisture can evaporate from the flowers.

The sand does not actually absorb the water from the flowers. Sand is used to hold the flowers in natural positions while they are drying. The flowers will lose their water through simple evaporation. Drying time is approximately three to five weeks, depending on room temperature, humidity, the number and thickness of flowers.

FRAGRANT DRIED FLOWERS

Dried flowers can easily be made fragrant by putting about 3 drops of oil on each flower head. You can use a single type of scented oil or a combination of scented oils. There are some combinations of two oils that have proven to work well together. Here are a few: lavender and rose, rose and clove, lavender and lemon, and mandarin and orange blossom.

Simply add your choice of scented oil to the
flower heads and place them in a plastic bag for
24 hours. This acts as a cure for the scent and
will preserve the fragrance for a longer period of
time.

DRY POTPOURRI

Dry potpourri is the easiest potpourri to make.
It is made from a mixture of dried flowers and
herbs which give it an attractive appearance
and subtle fragrance. Dry potpourri does not
require special equipment to make, so it is a
popular way to begin potpourri making.

USING FLOWERS AND HERBS
Dry potpourri can be made from most kinds of
aromatic herbs and fragrant flowers. You can
experiment with different combinations to find
your favorites and the ones suited for particular
occasions, or even different locations in the home
or office.

You can harvest flowers and herbs any time
throughout the year and save them until enough
are collected and you're ready to make
potpourri. Dry the flowers and herbs and store
in air tight containers or plastic bags until
needed. Any flowers that you do not grow in
the garden can be purchased at the store. Also,

flowers from arrangements can be saved to add to a potpourri mix.

Add fresher flowers to a dull looking potpourri mix to give it a more attractive appearance.

EQUIPMENT AND INGREDIENTS

Most kitchens have all the equipment you will need for making dry potpourri. The items you will use are scales and measuring spoons to measure ingredients for recipes, a mortar and pestle for crushing, a large mixing bowl, and air tight containers or plastic bags to cure the potpourri.

In addition to equipment, you will need ingredients other than herbs and flowers. Such ingredients are mixed in to give the potpourri a long lasting fragrance.

Spices, fragrant wood shavings, and citrus peels can be added to complement the flower and herb scents. Scented oils provide a stronger fragrance to enhance the aroma of the potpourri mixture. Fixatives are included in the mixture to help preserve the fragrance of other ingredients and to provide complementary scents of their own.

A BASIC DRY POTPOURRI MIXTURE

Here is a basic guide for making dry potpourri. The proportions and ingredients are a standard for making fragrant and appealing-to-look-at potpourri. Of course you can vary and experiment with ingredients and combinations to make favorite recipes. This guide will get you started.

•**3 cups main fragrance flower,** this is the foundation of the mixture, a main flower like lavender or orange blossom.

•**1/2 to 1 cup herbs and leaves,** scent should complement the main fragrance flower.

•**Up to 6 TB spices, crushed,** to provide underlying scents to complement flowers and herbs.

•**3 to 4 TB dried citrus peel, crushed,** also complementary scents of flowers and herbs.

•**1 1/2 oz. orris root powder or other fixative,** to preserve scents of ingredients.

•**Up to 6 drops scented oils,** to enhance overall aroma of mixture, vary drops of oil depending on strength.

To make, place main fragrance flower and herb leaves into mixing bowl. Crush spices, citrus peels, and fixative with pestle and mortar. Some fixatives like orris root require grating. Grate if necessary. Mix crushed and grated ingredients with flowers and herbs.

Add scented oils, 1 drop at a time, and mix between drops. Vary the amount of scented oil according to strength of scent. If the mixture begins to take on a strong fragrance stop adding oil. Too much scented oil can dominate a mixture and ruin it. It is better to add more oil later if needed.

Place potpourri mixture into an air tight container or plastic bag. Store in cool, dry, and dark place for 6 weeks. Shake mixture every other day. During the storage period the scents of the ingredients will mix together to form an appealing fragrance.

THE BASIC INGREDIENTS
Potpourri can be made with a small variety of ingredients. You simply change ingredient combinations to create interesting and attractive aromas and appearances. To get started, begin with a small collection of ingredients.

The following is a list of basic ingredients to choose from to enable you to make many different combinations of mixtures.

FLOWERS AND HERBS
Rose petals, carnations, wallflowers, orange blossom, honeysuckle, lilac, nicotiana, peony, stocks, lavender, lemon verbena, chamomile, marigold, hydrangea, cornflower, mallow,

borage, delphinium, pansies, poppy petals, nasturtiums, salvia, zinnias, thyme, marjoram, peppermint, bay, and rosemary.

SPICES, OILS, AND OTHER INGREDIENTS

Cloves, cinnamon sticks, whole nutmeg, allspice berries, blade mace, vanilla pods, dried orange peel, sandalwood chips or powder, orris root powder. Rose, lavender, peppermint, orange, lemon, cedarwood, carnation, orange blossom oils.

There are many other ingredients available to grow or purchase to enhance your potpourri. As you become more experienced, or use the recipes that call for ingredients other than those listed above, experiment with different combinations.

POTPOURRI RECIPES

Here are recipes to get you started. Use them as is or change to suit your taste or availability of ingredients.

BASIC POTPOURRI

6 oz rose petals
1 oz any decorative flower
1 oz lemon verbena leaves
1 oz bay leaves, crumbled
6 inch cinnamon stick, crushed
1 oz dried orange peel
1 oz orris root powder
2 drops rose oil
2 drops lemon oil

SPICY ROSE POTPOURRI

2 cups dried rose petals
1/4 cup dried lavender flowers
1/4 cup lemon verbena
1/2 tsp ground cloves
1/2 tsp. orange blossom
1/2 tsp ground allspice
1 TB grated dried orange peel
2 tsp orris root
2 drops oil of lavender flowers
2 drops oil of roses

LAVENDER ROSE POTPOURRI

4 cups dried rose buds
1 cup lemon verbena
1 cup dried lavender flowers
finely grated peel of 1 orange
finely grated peel of 1 lemon
1 tsp ground allspice
1/2 tsp ground cloves
3 drops lavender oil
3 drops rose oil
1 TB orris root
1 TB gum benzoin

ROSE LAVENDER POTPOURRI

4 oz rose petals
2 oz   lavender flowers
1 oz marjoram
1 oz thyme
1 oz rosemary
2 TB orange peel, crushed
2 TB cloves, crushed
1 TB nutmeg, crushed
1 TB allspice berries, crushed
1 oz orris root powder
2 drops rose oil
2 drops orange blossom oil
1 drop clove oil

LEMON AND LAVENDER POTPOURRI

2 oz Lemon verbena
3 oz Lavender flowers
1 oz peppermint
1 oz marjoram
blue flowers for decoration(pansy, hydrangea)
1/2 whole nutmeg, ground
1 TB blade mace, crushed
1 oz orris root powder
2 drops lavender oil
1 drop lemon oil
1 drop orange blossom oil
1 drop peppermint oil

MARIGOLD ROSE POTPOURRI

4 oz rose petals
2 oz   dried marigolds
l oz bay leaves, crumbled
l oz sandalwood chips, bruised
l oz dried orange peel
2 drops cedarwood oil
2 drops carnation oil
l drop clove oil

YLANG YLANG ROSE POTPOURRI

4 oz rose petals
l oz basil
l oz jasmine flowers
l oz hibiscus flowers
l TB cardamom seeds, crushed
2 TB coriander seeds, crushed
*l oz gum benzoin crystals, crushed, or gum
benzoin powder*
2 drops rose oil
2 drops ylang ylang oil
l drop patchouli oil

JASMINE ROSE POTPOURRI

l oz jasmine flowers
2 oz rose buds
l/2 oz peony petals
l oz calamus root, crushed or grated
2 TB sanderswood
l TB cloves, crushed
l TB juniper berries, crushed
l TB myrrh crystals, crushed, or myrrh powder
1 drop vanilla oil
2 drops jasmine oil
l drop rose oil

HIBISCUS AND PEONY POTPOURRI

4 oz rose petals
2 oz hibiscus flowers
2 oz nasturtiums
l oz peony petals
2 TB dried lime peel, crushed
l/2 oz dried orange peel, crushed
6 tonquin beans, grated or crushed
2 vanilla pods, chopped and crushed
l TB sweet cicely seeds, crushed
l/2 oz bayberry powder
l oz orris root powder
2 drops rose oil
3 drops French musk oil

SWEET LEMON POTPOURRI

1 oz lemon balm leaves
2 oz rose petals
1/2 oz basil
1/2 oz thyme
1/2 oz poppy petals
1/2 oz peony
1/2 oz dried orange peel, crushed
1 oz sandalwood chips
1 oz calamus root, crushed
1 TB juniper berries, crushed
1 TB blade mace, crushed
1 TB broken cassia bark
1 oz gum tragacanth powder
2 drops lemon balm oil
2 drops rose oil
2 drops orange oil

LEMON HERB POTPOURRI

1 TB lemon thyme
1 TB hyssop
2 TB marjoram
1 oz cloves, crushed
1/2 oz cinnamon sticks, crushed
1/2 oz orris root

SWEET MEADOW POTPOURRI

l oz chamomile
l oz woodruff
l oz meadowsweet
l oz marjoram
l oz hyssop
l 1/2 oz yellow everlasting flowers
l oz dried lemon peel, crushed
l nutmeg, grated
3 drops honeysuckle oil
2 drops lilac oil

FRESH SCENT POTPOURRI

l oz costmary
l oz tansy
l oz lavender
l oz peppermint
1/2 oz lemon-scented geranium leaves
1/2 oz mint-scented geranium leaves
1/2 oz bay leaves
1/2 oz rosemary
l oz orris root powder
1/2 oz lovage root, crushed
3 drops rosemary oil
2 drops lemon oil
2 drops patchouli oil

LAVENDER ROSEMARY POTPOURRI

4 TB lavender
2 TB rosemary
l oz lemon peel
l oz juniper berries, crushed
l oz allspice berries, crushed
1/2 oz orris root powder
2 drops vanilla oil

SWEET BASIL POTPOURRI

4 TB basil
l oz bassia bark
l oz coriander seeds, crushed
l oz cardamon seeds, crushed
l oz orange peel
1/2 oz orris root powder

SWEET BAGS

Here are a few recipes for sweet bags. Add ingredients to small material bags and place in linen drawers and cupboards to give them fragrance.

ROSY SWEET BAG

2 oz rose petals
l oz coriander seeds, crushed
l/2 oz orris root powder
l l/2 oz calamus root pieces, crushed

LAVENDER ROSE SWEET BAG

2 oz rose petals
l oz lavender
l oz hyssop
2 TB lime peel, crushed
2 TB blade mace, crushed
2 drops patchouli oil
2 drops vetiver oil

KEEP MOTHS AWAY SWEET BAG

1 oz costmary
1 oz lavender
1/2 oz lemon verbena
1 oz cloves, crushed
1/2 oz orris root powder

HERBAL SWEET BAG

1 oz rosemary
1 oz peppermint
1 oz lemon balm
1/2 oz lemon verbena
1 oz cinnamon sticks, crushed
1 oz cloves, crushed
1 oz caraway seeds, crushed
1 oz orris root powder
1 oz dried lemon peel, crushed

CHAPTER 6

YOGURT MADE
AT HOME

MAKING YOGURT WITH YOUR DEHYDRATOR

Yogurt made at home is easy to make. It is fun to experiment with a variety of flavors and recipes. You will find that home made yogurt and store bought yogurt will vary from each other in taste and consistency.

Yogurt purchased at the store usually has a sweet sour taste and a more gelatin consistency. Yogurt made at home usually will have a milk like taste and a stiffer consistency.

Store bought yogurt will maintain its consistency after stirring, while home made yogurt loses its thickness when stirred and becomes more liquid.

The type of milk and the bacterial strains used in making home made yogurt will change the flavor of the yogurt. You can use whole milk, skim milk, or any combination of the two to make yogurt. The tartness and thickness of yogurt will be affected not only by the type of milk, but also temperature and incubation length.

The more milk fat, the sweeter the yogurt will taste.   You can add sweet cream to the milk to give it a very sweet taste.

Yogurt is made by controlling the souring process of milk by adding bacteria that is normally present in unpasteurized milk.   The most commonly used strain is Lactobacillus bulgaricus, which is considered to produce the best flavors.

The bacteria can be added to milk using powdered starters purchased from a health food store. You may also use a couple of spoonfuls of store bought yogurt that is unpasteurized and without additives. You can tell if the yogurt is unpasteurized or without additives from the label on the yogurt container.

Yogurt cultures grow at temperatures between 105 and 110 degrees F..   The yogurt will not grow if the temperature falls below 90 degrees F., and will be destroyed if the temperature is higher than 115 degrees F.

Your Ronco Food Dehydrator can maintain the temperature at a constant level so yogurt cultures can be placed in them and simply left to incubate.

SIMPLE STEPS FOR MAKING YOGURT

1. Heat 4 cups of milk in a saucepan.

2. Remove the saucepan from the heat just before it begins to boil.

3. If using a powdered culture starter, use the amount prescribed in the directions on the package, and stir into the milk.

If you are using natural unpasteurized yogurt as a starter, stir two tablespoons into the milk.

4. Pour the yogurt mix into small containers with lids. Each container should hold a serving size for one to two people. Margarine cups with lids are ideally sized for holding yogurt.

5. Put lids on the containers and place on the top shelf of the Ronco Food Dehydrator for incubating. You should insert at least 3 trays in the Food Dehydrator and place the yogurt containers on the top tray only.

6. Leave the yogurt to incubate for 8 hours. It is important that the yogurt not be disturbed during this time. Jogging or stirring could cause the yogurt to separate.

7. After 8 hours the yogurt is finished and should be refrigerated immediately.   After several hours of refrigeration it is ready for serving.

Yogurt stored in the refrigerator generally   will keep in good condition for about two weeks. Unopened containers will keep a little while longer if stored upside down to prevent air from entering them.

When cooking with yogurt, you get the best results by using low heat for short periods of time.

If possible, wait until the food is ready to be taken away from the heat before adding the yogurt. If the recipe calls for yogurt to be added at the beginning, mix a small amount of water blended with flour or cornstarch with the yogurt to stabilize it. This will prevent the yogurt from separating or curdling during the cooking process.

HELPFUL HINTS
You can maintain the thick consistency of yogurt by folding it into other ingredients rather than stirring it in.

Boil the reconstituted powdered milk 1 minute for a firmer curd.

Add 1 to 3 tablespoons of carrot or tomato juice to each quart of milk for a firmer curd.

Add 1 to 3 tablespoons of milk powder to each quart of milk for a finer curd.

For a smoother flavor when using skim milk alone, add about 10 percent whole milk to the skim milk.

For a very sweet, creamy yogurt, add 1/4 cup light sweet cream per quart of whole milk.

To make yogurt of any color simply add food coloring when mixing the starter with the milk.

TO FLAVOR YOGURT

Flavor can be added before or after the milk has coagulated. Adding flavor prior to coagulum can cause the curd to separate from the whey. This may slow down the coagulation process or sometimes prevent it from happening. When such difficulties arise, double-check to make certain your starter is alive. Try making some unflavored yogurt. If the starter appears to be alive, try doubling the amount of starter and add milk proportionally as needed and/or reduce amount of flavoring.

To add flavoring material after the milk has coagulated you must always stir the curd.   This tends to convert it to buttermilk.   You can avoid this by mixing dissolved, clear gelatin in with the flavoring.   When the gelatin stiffens, the yogurt will stiffen.   With this method, there is little flavoring material that can not be successfully added to the yogurt.

Beginning on the following page are easy to make flavored yogurt recipes to enjoy and have fun with.

FLAVORED YOGURTS

VANILLA YOGURT

4 1/4 cups milk
4 inch piece vanilla bean
1/2 cup sugar
1 tsp unflavored yogurt

Split the vanilla bean lengthwise in half and heat with the milk. Remove from heat just before boiling and let cool to 105 to 110 degrees F. Use a thermometer for accurate temperature. Take the vanilla bean halves out. Add yogurt and sugar and stir lightly. Pour yogurt mix into containers with lids. Incubate in Food Dehydrator until firm, approximately 6 to 10 hours. Refrigerate before serving. Makes 4 1/4 cups.

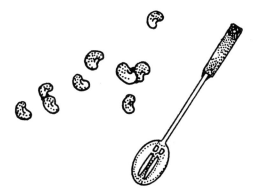

FRUIT JUICE YOGURT

3 1/2 cups milk,whole or skim
1/2 cup milk powder
2 TB yogurt
1/2 cup fruit juice, any kind

Mix ingredients and incubate in Food Dehydrator until firm, approximately 6 to 10 hours. Refrigerate for several hours before serving. Serves 4.

SPICED APPLES

1 lb. tart apples
1/4 cup brown sugar
1 tsp cinnamon
1/4 cup wine or dry sherry
6 TB butter
1/4 cup yogurt

Cut apples into thick slices and cook in heated butter, stirring constantly. When soft and light brown, add sugar, cinnamon, and wine. Cook mixture for 5 minutes. Remove from heat and spoon in yogurt, stir gently. Serve hot or cold. Serves 4.

<u>YOGURT FRUIT CUPS</u>

4 1/4 cups milk
1 TB unflavored yogurt
1 to 2 TB jam or jelly

Heat milk in a pan until just about boiling. Remove from heat and let cool to 105 to 110 degrees F. Use a thermometer for accurate temperature. Spread 1 to 2 tablespoons of jam or jelly on the bottom of 6 cup sized containers. Pour the milk and yogurt mixture over the jam or jelly to fill container. Cover and incubate in Food Dehydrator until firm, approximately 6 to 10 hours. Refrigerate for several hours before serving. Serves 6.

<u>FRESH FRUIT YOGURT</u>

1/2 cup fresh fruit or berries
honey or sugar to taste
1 quart milk
1 TB yogurt

Scald milk, let cool to lukewarm. Mix all ingredients and incubate in Food Dehydrator until firm, approximately 6 to 10 hours. Refrigerate for several hours before serving. 6 to 8 servings.

FRUIT-FLAVORED YOGURT

1 quart milk,whole or skim
3 TB milk powder
2 TB yogurt
2 TB fruit flavoring

Mix ingredients and incubate in Food Dehydrator until firm, approximately 6 to 10 hours. Refrigerate for several hours before serving. 6 to 8 servings.

FRUIT JUICE YOGURT

1/2 cup grape juice
1 cup apple juice
2 TB yogurt
1/4 cup raisins

Mix all ingredients in blender until smooth and creamy. Chill before serving. Makes 2 cups.

RASPBERRY YOGURT

4 cups yogurt, drained
1 cup raspberries

Mix yogurt and raspberries. Chill before serving. Serves 4.

SWEET APRICOT YOGURT

2 cups apricot nectar
4 cups yogurt
4 tsp honey

Mix apricot nectar and yogurt. Chill. Before serving sprinkle honey over mixture. Serves 4. Can substitute: Peach, pear, orange, apple, pineapple, grape juice.

STRAWBERRY SODA YOGURT

l cup sliced strawberries
l cup club soda
l cup yogurt
2 TB honey

Mix in blender until smooth. Chill. Serves 2.

DATE SMOOTHY

1 cup nonfat yogurt
1 cup milk
4 ice cubes
1 small ripe banana
6 pitted dates
2 TB honey
4 almonds

Mix all ingredients in a blender until smooth.
Serves 2.

BLOODY MARY

1 cup yogurt
2 cups tomato juice
1 tsp salt
1 tsp paprika
4 dashes worcestershire sauce

Mix ingredients in blender for 20 to 30 seconds.
Chill. Serves 2.

COFFEE YOGURT

1 quart   weak coffee
2 cups milk powder
2 TB yogurt
1 TB sugar, or sweeten to taste

Mix ingredients and incubate in Food Dehydrator until firm, 6 to 10 hours. Refrigerate several hours before serving. 6 to 8 servings.

COFFEE YOGURT PARFAIT

3 (8 oz) glasses   milk
1 (8-oz) glass sweet cream
3 TB milk powder
2 TB yogurt
4 TB honey, or sweeten to taste
4 tsp coffee

Mix ingredients and incubatein Food Dehydrator until firm, approximately 6 to 10 hours. Refrigerate several hours before serving. Serves 6 to 10.

<u>ALMOND ICE CREAM</u>

1 envelope unflavored gelatin
1 cup pineapple juice
1 cup orange juice
juice of 1 lemon
1 1/2 cups honey
1 1/2 cups drained yogurt
1/2 tsp almond extract
1/4 tsp salt
1/2 cup toasted slivered almonds
1 cup cream, whipped

Before starting, turn freezer control to coldest temperature. Pour pineapple juice into pan and stir in gelatin, honey and heat until all dissolved. Let cool. Blend rest of ingredients except whipped cream and mix with pineapple mixture. Spoon in whip cream. Pour into freezing tray and freeze until firm. Serves 6 to 8.

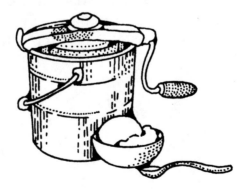

YOGURT POPSICLES

*1 can (6 oz) frozen orange, grape, or apple juice
concentrate
1 can (6 oz) water
1 cup unflavored yogurt*

Mix all ingredients thoroughly in a blender. Pour into popsicle cups or very small paper cups. Freeze, insert popsicle sticks when firm enough to hold them upright. Fully freeze. Makes 8 popsicles.

CHOCOLATE YOGURT

*2 TB yogurt
1 quart whole milk
3 TB milk powder
2 TB standard chocolate syrup*

Mix ingredients and incubate in Food Dehydrator until firm, approximately 6 to 10 hours. Refrigerate for several hours before serving. Serves 6 to 8.

CARAMEL YOGURT

6 TB honey
3 TB black strap molasses
l quart milk
l TB yogurt

Mix ingredients and incubate in Food Dehydrator until firm, approximately 6 to 10 hours. Refrigerate several hours before serving.   Serves 6 to 8.

CAROB YOGURT

1 quart milk
6 TB carob powder
honey to taste
l TB yogurt

Mix   carob, honey, and milk, scald.   Cool until lukewarm.   Add yogurt and incubate   in Food Dehydrator until firm, approximately 6 to 10 hours.   Refrigerate several hours before serving. Serves 6 to 8.

AVOCADO ICE CREAM

1 large avocado, peeled and seeded
1 cup yogurt
1/2 cup powdered milk
1/4 cup honey
1/3 cup lemon juice
rind of 1 lemon

Mix ingredients in a blender until smooth.
Freeze in freezing tray. Stir a few times while
freezing.

YOGURT MAIN DISHES

ARTICHOKES WITH YOGURT HOLLANDAISE

2 TB lemon juice
2 TB salt
6 globe artichokes
Sauce:
1 TB lemon juice
salt to taste
freshly ground black pepper to taste
1/2 cup butter
4 egg yolks
1/2 cup unflavored yogurt

Place artichokes, lemon juice and salt in pot of boiling water about 4 inches deep. Reduce heat, cover and simmer until artichokes are cooked, approximately 30 to 45 minutes. Place artichokes upside down and let drain. Spread leaves away from the middle, pull out leaves in center and the hairy choke.

Sauce: Add lemon juice, salt, pepper, butter, egg yolks to top of double boiler when bottom boiler is close to boiling. Stir briskly. When the mixture begins to thicken, reduce heat and add yogurt. Stir until sauce is thick and light. Serve with warm artichokes. Serves 6.

AVOCADO GAZPACHO

4 1/4 cups light chicken stock
1 medium onion, chopped
1 small green pepper, deseeded and chopped
1/2 cucumber, peeled and chopped
1 large, ripe avocado, peeled, pitted and chopped
1/4 cup tomatoes
2/3 cup unflavored yogurt
1 TB wine vinegar
salt to taste
freshly ground black pepper to taste
cayenne pepper to taste

Mix in blender all ingredients except seasonings. Blend until smooth. Season to taste. Pour soup mixture into serving bowl and chill cold before serving. Serves 6.

CHICKEN IN TARRAGON SAUCE

4 boneless chicken breasts
l/4 cup butter
l medium onion, finely chopped
l clove garlic, finely chopped
l l/4 cups chicken stock
l TB chopped fresh tarragon or l tsp dried
l l/4 cups unflavored yogurt
l TB cornstarch
2 egg yolks
salt and freshly ground black pepper to taste

Dry the chicken breasts with paper towels. Melt the butter in saute dish. When it froths, add the chicken. Brown the chicken breasts on both sides and transfer to a warm dish. Keep warm.

Add onion and garlic to saute dish, and simmer on low heat until the onion is soft but not browned.   Add chicken stock and tarragon, bring to a boil. Return the chicken pieces to saute dish, lower the heat, and simmer until the chicken is cooked,   approximately 10 minutes. Transfer the chicken to a serving dish and keep warm. Combine yogurt, cornstarch and egg yolks, stir gently.   Slowly add the yogurt mixture to the liquid in the saute dish, stirring continuously. Simmer until the mixture thickens.   Season to taste.   Serves 4.

BEEF STROGANOFF

1 lb. steak
1/4 cup butter
1 onion, finely chopped
1 clove garlic, minced
1/2 lb mushrooms, thinly sliced
2 TB dry sherry
1 tsp Dijon mustard
2/3 cup unflavored yogurt
2/3 cup sour cream
2 TB cornstarch
salt to taste
freshly ground black pepper to taste
fresh dill or parsley for garnish

Trim steak, beat it flat, and cut into narrow short strips. Saute onion and garlic in 2 tablespoons of butter until soft and starting to brown. Add mushrooms and simmer on very low heat while turning mushrooms. Transfer the vegetables to a dish and keep warm.

Add the rest of the butter to pan, add steak and brown. Reduce heat and add vegetables, dry sherry, and mustard. Add yogurt and cornstarch, and heat until sauce becomes hot and thick. Season to taste. Fold in sour cream just before serving and garnish with fresh dill or parsley. Serves 4-6.

SEAFOOD PIE

1/4 cup butter
1/4 cup flour
1 1/4 cups milk
2/3 cup unflavored yogurt
2/3 cup white wine or chicken stock
3/4 lb cooked white fish, flaked
1/4 lb cooked shelled shrimp
1/4 lb cooked white crab meat
1/4 lb cooked scallops, diced
2 TB chopped scallions
1/4 tsp curry powder (optional)
salt to taste
freshly ground black pepper to taste
3/4 lb frozen puff pastry
1 egg, beaten

Melt butter in a pan and stir in flour. Cook for a couple of minutes without letting it brown. Stir in milk, yogurt, and wine. Simmer on low heat for 2 minutes. Add fish, shrimp, crab, scallops, scallions, and seasonings. Pour into pie pan and let cool.

Thaw, roll pastry and cut out a narrow strip to line the pie pan edge. Moisten the pan lip with water and lay the strip along the edge. Use egg to dampen the pastry strip and cover it and the pie with pastry. Mound the edge and make a slit in middle of pie for releasing heat pressure.

Brush only the top with egg and bake in preheated oven at 425 degrees F. for 35 minutes until golden brown. Serves 4 to 6.

YOGURT FISH CAKES

2 cups cooked fish
l green pepper, minced
l onion, minced
2 TB butter
l TB minced parsley
l l/2 cups yogurt
3 l/2 cups hot mashed potatoes
l egg, beaten
chopped chives

Saute pepper and onion in butter for 2 minutes. Remove from heat and add fish, parsley and yogurt. Mix egg with mashed potatoes and pour half of potato mixture into baking dish. Spread all of fish mixture over potatoes. Top with remaining potatoes and garnish with chopped chives. Bake 15 to 20 minutes in 350 degree oven. Serves 6.

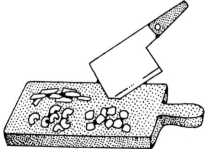

SEA SCALLOPS

1 1/2 lbs. scallops
1 1/2 cups dry sherry
salt and pepper
2 TB canola oil
1 TB butter
1 TB flour
1 cup yogurt
1/2 cup milk
1/2 cup chopped mushrooms
2 TB grated Swiss cheese
2 TB bread crumbs
fresh dill or parsley for garnish

Mix scallops, sherry, salt and pepper in large pan. Cover, and slowly bring to boil over low heat. Simmer for 5 minutes. Drain liquid and set aside. Chop scallops and set aside. Pour mixture into buttered casserole dish, sprinkle on bread crumbs. Heat in broiler until golden brown. Garnish with dill or parsley. Serves 4 to 6.

COD FISH WITH MUSHROOMS

2 lbs. cod fish, fillets or steaks
6 TB canola or corn oil
1/4 lb. mushroom caps, thinly sliced
1/4 cup butter
1 cup yogurt
1 TB flour
salt

Put oil in baking pan. Sprinkle salt on fish and add fish to oil in pan. Turn fish to coat with oil on both sides. Bake at 400 degrees until tender. Saute butter and mushrooms until soft. After fish has cooked, cover with mushrooms. Stir flour and yogurt together in a dish until smooth. Then cover fish and mushrooms with yogurt mixture. Place in oven and cook for 15 minutes. Serves 4 to 6.

<u>YOGURT DRESSINGS</u>

<u>YOGURT MAYONNAISE</u>

4 egg yolks
1/2 tsp dry mustard
pinch salt
pinch freshly ground black pepper
l tsp lemon juice
l l/4 cups olive oil
l l/4 cups unflavored yogurt

Allow ingredients to stand until they become room temperature. Put egg yolks, mustard, salt and pepper in medium bowl. Whisk to a smooth paste. Add lemon juice and whisk until smooth again. Add olive oil, one drop at a time, while vigorously beating mixture. After 1/4 cup of oil has been added, slowly pour rest of oil in thin stream. Add yogurt slowly while beating.

Season to taste. Cover bowl and refrigerate before serving. If sealed air tight, yogurt mayonnaise will keep about one week in refrigerator.

BLUE CHEESE YOGURT DRESSING

1 TB finely chopped onion
1/2 cup crumbled Roquefort cheese
1 cup unflavored yogurt
1/2 tsp lemon juice
freshly ground white pepper to taste

Combine all ingredients in blender and mix until smooth. Refrigerate well before serving. Makes 1 1/4 cup.

AVOCADO YOGURT DRESSING

1 ripe avocado, peeled, seeded
1 TB lime juice
2/3 cup unflavored yogurt
2 TB picante sauce
salt to taste

Combine ingredients in blender and mix until smooth. Season to taste. Use immediately. Makes 1 1/4 cups.

YOGURT SALADS

FRUIT SLAW

1 lb hard white cabbage, shredded
2   carrots, grated
2 crisp   apples, grated
3 TB dates
3 TB coarsely chopped walnuts
2/3 cup yogurt mayonnaise
1 tsp sugar
salt to taste
freshly ground black pepper to taste

Combine ingredients in bowl and mix thoroughly. Chill for 1 to 2 hours. Serves 4 to 6.

SWEET FRUIT SALAD

1 small fresh pineapple
l cup mango chunks or melon balls
l cup diced papaya, peaches or nectarines
2 cups yogurt
2 TB honey
l cup sliced strawberries
1 cup grapes
4 sprigs fresh mint

Quarter pineapple lengthwise, and core. Set aside empty shell in refrigerator. Slice pineapple into cubes and toss 1 cup pineapple with mango, papaya and grapes. Chill. To serve put 1/3 cup of yogurt into each pineapple shell, cover with mixed fruit. Mix remaining yogurt with honey and cover fruit. Top with strawberries. Use one whole strawberry and one sprig to garnish each shell. Serves 4.

<u>SWEET APPLE MEDLEY</u>

3 big apples, finely chopped
2 TB honey or brown sugar
1 TB lemon juice
1/2 cup chopped dates or raisins
1/2 cup chopped nuts
1 cup yogurt
1/2 cup diced celery
1/2 cup shredded coconut

Mix honey, lemon juice, dates, nuts and celery. Fold in apples and yogurt.   Garnish with shredded coconut.   Serves 4.

CALIFORNIA FRUIT SALAD

1 1/2 cups yogurt
2 TB orange marmalade
1 large grapefruit, sectioned
1 large orange, sectioned
1 nectarine, sectioned
1 avocado, sliced lengthwise
romaine or greens
seedless white grapes

Chill grapes. Put orange marmalade and yogurt into blender and whip smooth. Arrange avocado, oranges, grape fruit, and nectarines on lettuce leaves. Cover with yogurt mixture and garnish with grapes. Serves 6.

BANANA SPLIT SALAD

1 cup yogurt
1/2 cup crushed pineapple, drained
1 TB honey
4 bananas, peeled
1/4 cup chopped nuts
1/2 cup crushed strawberries
4 maraschino cherries

Mix yogurt, pineapple and honey. Cut bananas lengthwise in half. Use 2 banana halves for each serving . Put 1/4 cup yogurt mixture on each serving. Sprinkle with nuts, and top with strawberries. Garnish with cherries. Serves 4.

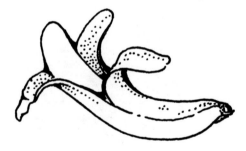

YOGURT BREADS AND CAKES

PUFF FRIED BREAD

3 cups whole-wheat flour
1 tsp salt
1/2 cup butter
1 1/2 cup yogurt

Mix ingredients well and knead until smooth.
Form into balls, roll into thin flat cakes. Fry in
deep fat at 380 degrees until puffed and brown.
Serve hot.

<u>RICE CAKES</u>

1 egg, beaten
2 TB margarine, melted
1 cup cooked rice
1 1/2 cups yogurt
1 cup flour, sifted
2 TB sugar
1/2 tsp salt
3/4 tsp baking soda
1/2 cup milk

Mix egg, yogurt, margarine and rice. Add the rest of the ingredients, and stir until mixed well. Fold onto hot oiled griddle. Brown both sides. Serve plain or with syrup. Makes 18   3 inch cakes.

YOGURT WAFFLES

2 cups sifted white flour (or 2/3 cups whole
wheat flour with 1 1/3 cup white flour)
3 tsp baking powder
1 tsp baking soda
1 tsp salt
2 cups yogurt
4 eggs, separated
1 cup melted butter or margarine

Preheat waffle iron. Mix flour, baking soda, and
salt. Blend yogurt, butter, and egg yolks
separately, then add to flour mixture. Mix at
high speed until smooth. Beat egg whites stiff,
and fold into batter. Bake in waffle iron. Makes
6 to 8 waffles.

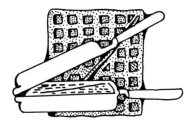

CHAPTER 7

FACTS ABOUT STORING

HOW TO RECONSTITUTE DRIED FOODS

During the dehydrating process water is dried out of the fruits and vegetables. Dried food can be eaten in its dried form, or we can put the water back into the produce which is called reconstituting, rehydrating, or refreshing.

When vegetables are served alone as a side dish they need to be reconstituted to freshen them up. Fruits that are cooked or baked as part of a recipe also need to be rehydrated.

Dried food is less bulky than fresh produce. You use about one-fourth to one-half the amount of dried food as you would fresh produce in your recipes.

If dehydrated food is properly pretreated by either steam or water blanching, only a minimum amount of time is required for rehydrating.

Dried vegetables make excellent ingredients in soups, sauces, stews, stuffings, and casseroles. Dried fruits are great when used to make bread, pies, puddings, and cobblers.

There are two ways to reconstitute fruits and vegetables; by soaking in cold water or by pouring boiling water over the food and soaking .

It is generally faster and the results tend to be better by using boiling water.   Use the least amount of water possible to prevent the leeching of nutrients.   Following are instructions for each method.

TO RECONSTITUTE WITH COLD WATER

Place dried food in a pot and cover with cold water.   The amount of water needed varies with the type of fruit or vegetable.   The chart below gives amounts of water and suggested soaking times.   For cold water the soaking time may be a little longer.

It is a good idea to use half the amount of water to start with, soak the food and add water as needed.   Soak until the fruit or vegetables resemble their original texture.

RECONSTITUTING WITH BOILING WATER

Place the fruits or vegetables in a pot and pour enough boiling water over them to just cover the dried food. (It does not work as well to put the dried food into a pot with boiling water.) Water should be added as needed.   See chart below for suggested water amount and soaking time.

Cover the pot with a lid and place pot on low heat.   The heat should not be hot enough to simmer.   Turn off heat after five minutes and allow food to soak until texture looks like fresh produce.

RECONSTITUTION TABLE

Food	Suggested Hot Water per cup of Dried Food (cups)		Soaking Time (Hours)
Apples....................	1	1/2	1 / 2
Asparagus	2	1/4	1 1/2
Beans, lima	2	1/2	1 1/2
Beans....................	2		1
Beets....................	2	3/4	1 1/2
Carrots..................	2	1/4	1
Cabbage...............	3		1
Corn.....................	2 1/4		1/2
Okra	3		3 / 4
Onions	2		3 / 4
Peaches.................	2		1
Pear.....................	1	3/4	3 / 4
Peas	2	1/2	1 / 2
Pumpkin	3		1
Squash...................	1	3/4	1
Spinach.................	1		1 / 2
Sweet potatoes.......	1	1/2	1 / 2
Turnips.................	1		3 / 4

The water used for reconstituting will have many nutrients left over from the fruit or vegetables and will be full of flavor. Whenever possible use it to cook with or add to other foods.

PASTEURIZING

Pasteurizing is a method of treating food after it has been dried to further reduce the risk of spoilage or insect contamination.   Before storing food you may want to pasteurize.

If food was properly dried with a home dehydrator it may not need pasteurizing, but it doesn't hurt.   It is a must to pasteurize food that was dried outdoors or if you plan to keep food stored for more than six months .

There are two ways to pasteurize food.   You can freeze it or heat it.   To pasteurize by freezing, place the food in plastic bags or containers and keep it for at least 48 hours at a temperature below zero degrees F.

Freezing is the optimal way to pasteurize because fewer nutrients are destroyed. Maintaining a temperature below zero can only be done with an upright or a chest freezer.   The freezer in your kitchen refrigerator will not maintain that low a temperature.

Heating is an alternative to freezing.   To heat pasteurize, place the food in the oven for 10 to 15 minutes at 175 degrees F.   It should be layered no more than 1 inch thick on trays.   Let the pieces cool before storing.

STORAGE

After pasteurizing, immediately pack the food for storage. Dried food will soon begin to draw moisture from the air if not stored quickly. So when storing dried food in the refrigerator, even for a short period of time, put it in an airtight container. This is important as the refrigerator's cool air is filled with moisture that the dried produce will quickly soak up.

A sterile airtight container is a must for food storage. Glass jars, plastic bags, and plastic containers are suitable. Even metal cans can be used as long as the food is put into plastic or paper so it does not touch the metal.

When storing food in clear containers, line them with colored paper so food is not exposed to damaging light. If possible, always store where it is dark.

Even though you may have dried combinations of food types together, store each food type in separate containers. This keeps the foods from acquiring the fragrance and flavor of each other.

Store meal sized portions in smaller individual bags. This makes it easy to use only the amount you will need at one time, and if there is any spoilage it would be limited to a small portion rather than contaminating a whole batch.

Check the food from time to time for moisture or spoilage.   If after the first couple of days there is moisture, you cannot dry the food again and it should be thrown out.   If mold is present on food at any time, throw out all of the pieces that shared the same container.

A simple and cost effective technique to prevent moisture from spoiling the fruit is to line the bottom of containers with half an inch of kitty litter.   It may sound like an odd idea, but kitty litter is merely concrete that has been crushed and cleaned.   Only use the plain kind which does not have deodorizers or coloring added to it.

Kitty litter is clean, but   it is not food grade, so be sure the food does not come in contact with it. Place paper towels on top of the kitty litter, or use paper coffee filters which will fit nicely into glass jars.

While proper storage is essential to preserving food, it is equally important to scrutinize stored food before serving.   Check for any signs of spoilage, discoloration, or invasion of pests or insects.

Even with proper storage techniques there may be some food that must be discarded depending on time stored and conditions.   This is normal and part of the dried food process.   Proper preparation, drying, and storage steps will keep your food spoilage to a minimum and maximize the amount of tasty, nutritious food available long after it was fresh.

FREEZING VEGETABLES

Freezing, like drying and canning does not improve the taste and nutrition quality of food. As discussed earlier, only the highest quality and freshest produce should be used. Superior results will be achieved if the vegetables are also frozen when they are at their peak maturity or ripeness.

Vegetables are easy to prepare for freezing and are a popular freezer item because they retain so much of their original color, texture, and nutrients. Almost any vegetable can be frozen.

There are a few vegetables that do not freeze well. Some of these are salad greens, cabbage, whole tomatoes, and Irish potatoes. These vegetables lose their shape and/or texture when defrosted. This is because they have high water content and a large amount of ice crystals form in them.

Some varieties of vegetables are better suited to freezing than others. Check with your grocer and seed catalogs for vegetables in your area that will freeze the best.

Packing materials will affect the quality of frozen vegetables. All packing materials should keep the liquids and vapors inside the package and keep outside liquids and vapors from getting inside.

Packages should have as little air as possible inside them.   If air is inside, the food can oxidize which   will lead to the loss of flavor, nutrients, and food color.

Sealing of the packages is important for proper preserving of frozen food.   The seal must be moisture and vapor-proof.   Often it is the seal which allows air and moisture to seep into the package causing loss of flavor and nutrient quality.

The   optimum   freezer   temperature   is   zero degrees F.   If food is frozen too slowly or if the temperature fluctuates above five   degrees F., the size of the ice crystals will increase in the vegetables and negatively affect the quality and storage life.

A general rule of thumb is to freeze no more than two pounds of food per cubic foot capacity of your freezer (30 cubic foot = 60 lbs. of food). Packages should be spread evenly in the freezer.

GENERAL PREPARATION

Before cutting the vegetables, wash them with cold water. Make sure the vegetables do not pick up any dirt which has settled to the bottom of pans during the rinsing and holding process.

Soak the vegetables for half an hour in salt water to flush out any insects. Use one tablespoon of salt for each quart of cold water. The insects can be removed from the water as they float to the surface. Remove the salt from the produce by rinsing with cold water.

DRY PACK

The most popular method of freezing is to dry pack. It's the easiest way to freeze the vegetables. You simply cook the vegetables as if they were fresh. Dry packing simply means freezing without liquid.

An especially effective dry pack method is to quick freeze (20 degrees F.) the produce in a single layer on a tray. After they are frozen place the vegetables in containers and seal them. Because the pieces were frozen in a single layer they do not stick together. When cooking, this method allows you the convenience of only removing the amount of vegetables needed from the container. Any vegetables not needed can be left in the container, resealed, and put back into the freezer.

While most vegetables can be cooked without thawing, leafy vegetables should be allowed to defrost until the leaves separate before cooking. Corn on the cob should also be thawed before cooking because the cob will stay cold and keep the cooked corn from staying warm if it is not fully defrosted.

Vegetables can be cooked by boiling. To boil vegetables use 1/2 cup of water for every 2 cups of frozen vegetables. Boil until vegetables appear the desired texture of cooked fresh vegetables.

An alternative for cooking frozen vegetables is to bake them. Baking takes a little longer than boiling. It generally takes about 45 minutes to cook vegetables at 350 degrees F.

Vegetables that were cooked before they were frozen simply need to be heated to serving temperature.

FREEZING FRUITS

Try to select fruit which is at the very best stage of ripeness and flavor for freezing. If you are going to spend time freezing fruit, you want to have top quality fruit to serve after defrosting it.

It is best to work with only small batches of fruit. A good rule of thumb is to work with two to three quarts of fruit at a time.

Begin by rinsing the fruit in cold water. An effective method is to put the fruit into a mesh basket and dunk it into a tub or bucket of cold water. Peel, pit and prepare the fruit as you would for serving fresh fruit.

Cut pieces into serving size. Small fruits can be frozen whole or they can be crushed. A wire potato masher works well for crushing soft fruit. Firmer fruits can be put in a food chopper.

Blenders and food processors can be used to chop the produce or make puree, but watch closely and use for a minimum amount of time. It takes very little time to liquify the fruit. The best bet is to use a colander or strainer.

The next step is to simply put the prepared fruit into freezer containers and seal them, making sure they are air and vapor tight as discussed earlier.

When opening a frozen package to prepare for cooking, check the vegetables for natural color and texture appearance. Top quality food should have absolutely no freezer burn, and a minimum of ice crystals.

Here are some hints to help avoid loss of frozen food due to freezer or power failure.

Clean and dust the coils of the freezer once or twice a year according to your freezer's instruction manual. Check the freezer for any leakage, noises, or excessive running. If any are found, have the freezer repaired.

Make sure the coils have adequate clearance around them for air circulation and are not covered or blocked.

If you experience a power failure, do not open the freezer. This only speeds up the thawing process. Generally power failures only last a short time and a well packed freezer will keep food for many hours.

Mechanical failure of a freezer is often not discovered until the freezer is opened when searching for food to cook. If this happens, immediately check condition of the food. If the foods are still frozen, they can be saved.

If any of the food packages are warm or have thawed for more than two days, it should be thrown away. If there is any doubt whether the food has thawed or warmed too much, it is safest to discard it.

Once the condition of the food is known, act quickly to plan how to save it. If the freezer can not be repaired for more than a few hours, there are several alternatives.

Some of the frozen food can be stored in the kitchen freezer, and the rest can be moved to another freezer. Usually friends or family have extra space available, or there are local commercial freezers who will rent space.

To transport frozen food, place the packages in ice chests if possible or in cardboard boxes. Line the boxes with newspaper to act as insulation. Place the packages as close together as possible in the boxes.

An alternative method to save frozen food is to use dry ice. The frozen food can be left in the freezer and dry ice can be placed in the freezer to keep everything frozen.

Usually 25 to 50 pounds will work. Keep the dry ice as whole as possible and only break it up as necessary to fit in the freezer.

Precautions should be taken with dry ice. It can burn the skin if not handled with gloves. Dry ice gives off carbon dioxide as it evaporates which can cause unconsciousness. A well ventilated

room will keep the carbon dioxide from building
to a risky level. Simply crack open a window
near the freezer to allow ventilation of the room.
When transporting the dry ice in the car, also
keep a window cracked open.

CANNING
FRUITS & VEGETABLES

Preserving spring and summer's fruits and
vegetables can be a simple and enjoyable
experience. Canning can be an easy step by step
process if you do some planning and preparation,
and gather necessary equipment before actually
starting.

Most of the utensils and equipment you'll need
for canning are commonly found in the kitchen.
To help you get organized we have prepared a
list of items you will need.

CANNING UTENSILS AND EQUIPMENT
•Water bath canner and/or steam pressure
canner.
•6 to 8 quart kettle for precooking foods, should
be enamel or stainless steel.
•Glass canning jars with new closures, perfect
condition.
•Clock with alarm buzzer. Clock with sweeping
second hand or digital seconds displayed. Also a
one minute timer.

•Food thermometer, must be glass and pencil shaped.
•Shallow pans.
•Funnel with wide mouth.
•Ladle.
•Perforated ladle or long handled slotted spoon.
•Blender.
•Colander.
•Strainer.
•Measuring cups and spoons.
•Weight scales.
•Jar lifter.
•Juice strainer.
•Long handled fork.
•Large trays.
•Clean dish cloths, towels, pot holders.

There are two pieces of special equipment that are required to process canned food. One is a water bath canner which is used to process most food that is canned. Low acid foods, like vegetables and jellies, can not be processed with a water bath canner.

The other special canning equipment is a steam pressure canner. It is used for processing low acid foods, meats, poultry, and seafood.

WATER BATH CANNER
A water bath canner is used to process foods at boiling temperature (212 degrees F.) for a specific period of time to destroy spoiling agents like bacteria, mold, and yeast.

The food is actually sterilized inside the canning jars by the boiling bath water of the canner.

There are various types of water bath canners available to purchase. If you are going to buy a canner be sure to get one that can process both pint and quart sized jars. Not all canners are large enough, they must be 11 1/2 inches high to accomodate quart size jars.

The most common types of water bath canners are stainless steel, enamel, or aluminum. Stainless steel canners are relatively expensive. They require little maintenance, last a long time, are light weight and durable. Stainless steel canners also stay shiny and attractive after much use.

Enamelware canners are inexpensive, require low maintenance, and with tender care can provide long service. Enamelware canners do tend to chip easily. If they become heavily chipped they can not be used for canning. The metals below the enamel surface would leech out into the food during processing.

Aluminum water bath canners are inexpensive and durable. They do require extra maintenance to keep up their appearance because aluminum canners tend to darken and discolor.

By adding 1/4 cup of vinegar to the canning water bath, you can avoid some staining caused by hard water. To remove stains mix 1 to 2 tablespoons of cream of tarter per quart of water and boil the solution inside the canner for 5 to 10 minutes.

THE STEAM PRESSURE CANNER

The steam pressure canner is used to process low acid foods that require high temperature processing. Steam pressure canners can heat and maintain food temperatures at 240 degrees F. Such a high temperature is required to destroy the botulism toxin.

A steam pressure canner is a heavy weight kettle with a locking cover that allows steam pressure to be maintained at a constant level. Pressure canners come in various sizes.

The most popular size of pressure canner holds 7 quart sized jars or 10 pint sized jars. Before buying a large size pressure canner consider whether you have enough stove space to accomodate a large canner. Also, canners are heavy and difficult for one person to manage when they are full.

The two types of steam pressure canners available are the weighted gauge canner and the pressure dial canner. The weighted gauge canner has a gauge on its lid that uses weight to control the inside steam pressure. It is low maintenance and only requires cleaning after each use.

The dial pressure gauge canner has a gauge on the cover that measures pressure pounds inside the canner.   It has a petcock which can be opened to release pressure.   The dial gauge canner requires periodic maintenance to keep the pressure gauge reading accurately.   The dial gauge should be tested before each use.

Carefully follow the manufacturers directions for the pressure   canner you have .   For high altitudes be sure to follow the directions for adjusting to high altitudes.

PREPARING JARS FOR CANNING

Carefully inspect glass jars for imperfections that could prevent the jar from sealing properly. Look for chips, cracks, or dips in the rim of the jar. Try running your finger along the rim to feel for defects you may not see. Jars that have defects in them should not be used as they will not provide an airtight seal. If the jars are not airtight, food can not be properly canned.

The jars should be thoroughly washed in the hottest water possible. Use soap and a scrubbing brush to reach all parts of the jars. The jars can be washed in a dishwasher if very hot water is used.

After washing, place the jars upside down to drain. When dry, place them upside down on a clean towel or tray and cover with a towel to keep the dust and insects away.

If the jars will be used for canning immediately after washing, keep them in hot water until they are packed with food.

STERILIZING THE JARS

Sterilization is not necessary if a steam pressure canner or boiling bath process is used for canning. Both processes sterilize the jars and its contents at the same time.

Jars for packing jellies and storing dried foods must always be sterilized. Jars that have gotten

dirty, have been used to hold milk, or have held
spoiled food should also be sterilized.

To sterilize the glass jars, place them upside
down on a rack inside a kettle.   Fill the kettle
with water to cover the jars and boil them for a
minimum of 15 minutes.

If you live in an area with hard water, a film
may develop on the jars during sterilizing.   This
is caused by the minerals in the water and will
not harm food quality.   A half cup of vinegar
mixed with the water during sterilization usually
prevents film from forming on the jars.

REHEATING THE JARS
The jars should always be heated before hot or
cold food is packed into them.   There are a
number of ways to reheat the sterilized jars.

The jars can be placed in a kettle of water and
simmered on low heat, put into rinse and dry
cycles of the dishwasher, or simply rinsed under
hot water in the kitchen sink.   The glass jars can
also be placed in the water bath canner and let
stand in the preheated canning water.

HOT PACK AND RAW PACK METHODS
Once the jars are reheated, they can be packed. There are two ways of packing food into jars for canning, the hot pack and raw pack methods.

The hot pack method simply means that the food is heated or cooked before packing. Raw pack means the food is not heated or cooked before it is packed for canning.

HOW TO HOT PACK
With the hot pack method, you transfer the hot food from the kettle it was cooked in, to the heated canning jars. The kettle should not be removed from the heat until all the food has been packed.

Loosely pack the food into the jars making sure enough room is left for head space. See instructions in the head space section below.

Next, cover the food with the juices or syrup from the food cooked in the kettle. Maintain a proper head space and see that the food pieces are completely covered by juice or syrup.

If the food pieces are sticking up out of the juice or syrup, the air will cause them to turn dark.

HOW TO RAW PACK
With the raw pack method, the prepared but uncooked food is firmly packed into the heated canning jars. Leave enough head space according to the head space instructions.

Starchy foods tend to expand during the canning process.   Loosely pack starchy foods like lima beans, peas, corn, etc. to allow room for expansion.

Pour juice, syrup, or water over the food until the canning jar is filled and the pieces of food are covered.   Be sure head space is maintained.

REMOVING THE AIR BUBBLES
After packing the jars, use a thin nonmetal spatula to circle around the inside of the jar between the food and the glass.   This will release air bubbles that are trapped and let the liquid completely surround the food.

Make sure the food is completely covered with liquid on top, sides, and bottom.   Sometimes after the air bubbles are released, extra space is created.   If this happens, add more liquid to the jar to reach the proper amount of head space.

LEAVING HEAD SPACE

Head space is the amount of space that is left between the top of the packed food and the closure of the jar. The amount of space will vary depending on the food being canned. Use the recipe directions for the food you are canning to determine head space.

If there are no directions for head space, the following can be used:

Jellies, relishes, small size pickles	1/8 inch
Jams, preserves, large pickles, applesauce, butter, fruit purees	1/4 inch
Fruits, berries, beets, and tomatoes	1/2 inch
Vegetable, meats, and soup	1 inch

Head room space should be closely followed according to instructions. If there is too much head room, there will be too much air in the jar and the food could darken due to oxidation.

If there is too little head space, some of the liquid could be squeezed out by pressure during the canning process. Some of the food will be left uncovered and will oxidize.

CLOSING CANNING JARS

Both the canning jars and closures must be free of imperfections and able to hold an air tight seal. Carefully inspect them before each use.

There are two types of closures that are used on standard jars. One is a two piece closure that consists of a rubber ring and a porcelain lined zinc cap. The other type of closure has a two piece screw band and a flat self sealing lid.

If in perfect condition, the porcelain lined zinc cap and the two piece screw band can be repeatedly used. They must be in top quality condition and free of dents or rust.

The rubber rings and the self sealing flat lids can only be used once for canning. Always replace them even if they appear to be in good condition.

Following are instructions for using standard jars and the above closures. These instructions will not apply if you have jars with closures that are different.

CANNING WITH THE TWO PIECE SCREW BAND AND FLAT SELF SEALING LID.

The self sealing flat lids come with a sealing compound that must be softened with hot water. This is done by placing the lids into a pan and heating them in hot or boiling water depending on the brand (follow the manufacturer's instructions).

Heat the lids after the food is prepared, ready to pack, and the glass jars have been reheated. The lids should be left in the hot or boiling water until they are used.

Complete one jar and closure at a time. Each jar should be packed and sealed before moving to the next jar. Once you begin the canning process, do not stop until you have completed each jar one by one. Here are the steps.

1. Pack prepared food into jar.
2. Leave recommended head space.
3. Release air bubbles with a nonmetal spatula.
4. Wipe any food from rim of jar and threads.
5. Apply self sealing flat lid to rim of jar.
6. Screw the metal band firmly onto the jar. Hold the flat lid with one hand while screwing on the band with the other hand. Hand screw the band firmly. Do not use tools to tighten. Make sure the band does not cut through the sealing compound, and the lid is centered on jar.
7. Place jar in canner and begin packing the next jar.
8. Process the jars by following directions for the food you are canning.

After the canner processing is completed, turn the heat off, remove jars and place them upright on a towel or rack to cool. If a pressure cooker was used, allow the canner to decompress before removing the jars.

When the jars are removed from the canner, and begin to cool, there is usually a pleasing ping. It's a sound made by the lids as they seal.

If the screw band appears loose, do not tighten them after the jars have been removed from the canner.

Let the jars cool at room temperature in a draft free area. Keep at least one inch space between each jar. Do not place any type of cover over the group of jars while they are cooling. Let canned food stand for 12 to 24 hours.

After the jars have been allowed to cool completely, inspect the jars to make sure they are sealed. After removing the screw bands, check to see if the lid center is slightly concave or depressed. If properly sealed, the vacuum inside the jar will pull the center of the lid down.

Test to see if the lid can be lifted off the jar. Turn the jar on its side and rotate it slowly checking for leakage. If none is visible, and the lid is secure, the jar has sealed.

Place the canned food in a storage area that is cool, dark, and dry. Remember, light and heat are damaging to stored food.

CANNING WITH THE PORCELAIN LINED ZINC CAP AND RUBBER CLOSURE

After the food is prepared, ready to pack, and the jars are reheated, place the rubber rings into hot water to make them soft and pliable. Put all the rings on the heated jars at once.

Once all the jars have rings on them, pack and complete each jar one at a time. Here are the steps.

1. Place rubber rings on all jars.
2. Pack prepared food into jar.
3. Leave recommended head space.
4. Release air bubbles with a nonmetal spatula.
5. Wipe any food from rim of jar, threads, and rubber rings.
6. Immediately place the porcelain lined zinc cap on the jar. Tighten by hand as far as possible, then loosen just 1/4 inch.
7. Place jar in canner, begin packing the next jar.
8. Process the jars by following directions for the food you are canning.

Turn the heat off after canner processing is completed, remove jars. Tighten the closure cap with a canning wrench to completely seal them.

If a pressure canner was used, allow the canner to decompress before removing the jars. After taking the jars out of the pressure canner, tighten the closure caps with a canning wrench to completely seal them.

Let the jars cool at room temperature in a draft free area. Keep at least one inch between each jar. The group of jars should not be covered by any type of cloth or plastic cover while they are cooling. Let them cool for 12 to 24 hours.

The jar closures should not be adjusted or tightened once the jars have begun to cool. The seal could be broken if the closures are disturbed after the jars have cooled.

After the jars have been allowed to cool completely, inspect them to make sure they are sealed. Turn the jar on its side and rotate it slowly. Look for leakage. If none is present the jar has sealed.

TROUBLE SIGNS AFTER STORING

Before eating stored canned food, always inspect the jars carefully to make sure they are properly preserved. Below are signs that indicate food was not properly canned.

If any of these signs are present, <u>do not eat the canned food and destroy the food so it will not be eaten accidently by people or animals.</u>

<u>TROUBLE SIGNS</u>

- Bulging lids.
- Broken seals.
- Seepage around the seal.
- Mold in the contents, no matter how small.
- Mold on the seal, no matter how much.
- Mold on the inside of the jar, any at all.
- Unpleasant smell or odor in contents.
- Small bubbles inside the jar.
- Cloudy liquid.
- Liquid spurts out when jar is opened.
- Slimy consistency of the food.

GETTING ORGANIZED

You'll be a healthy, happy canner if you plan the canning process and organize your equipment, materials, and work area prior to the canning process. Here are steps to getting organized before starting the canning process.

1. Schedule free time for canning from start to finish. Make arrangements to avoid any

interruptions while you are canning. Let everyone know you will be busy and can not be disturbed. Then don't let anything interrupt you, not even the phone!

2. Make sure you or anyone else does not plan to cook during the time you are canning. You'll need the whole kitchen.

3. Organize equipment, materials, and food in advance. Test kitchen appliances, water bath canner, and/or pressure canner to make sure all are in ready condition and operating order.

4. Gather all utensils, kettles, ingredients, etc. that will be used. Plan how each will be used and place them where they will be convenient.

5. Go over the step by step canning procedures and read the recipes ahead of time. Plan to have them in a convenient spot during processing in case you need them. Do a "dry run" test of all the steps from start to finish to familiarize yourself with all the steps. This is a great way to discover overlooked equipment or materials.

6. Organize the work area. Give yourself plenty of space to work in. Place equipment and materials where they will be most handy. Plan for the preparation of the food, processing, cooking, and storing of the finished canned goods.

7. Have clean towels handy for wiping jars clean, and clean up materials for accidents or spills.

PREPARING FRUITS
Harvest fruits at their peak ripeness. Wash them thoroughly before any type of processing. Keep fruit cool before and during preparation.

Fruit should not be left to soak in water because water will leech the vitamins and flavor away. Pretreat light colored fruit with an antioxidant to keep them from darkening after they are sliced.

Antioxidants are used to preserve flavor as well as the color of fruit. Fruits can be treated with the antioxidants by dipping, sprinkling, or mixing the fruit with a syrup or sugar solution.

Ascorbic acid, which is vitamin C, is the most effective antioxidant for fruits. Ascorbic acid can be used in pure form, combined with citric acid, lemon juice, vinegar, or salt water.

Follow the recipe for the food you are canning to select the method and mixture of antioxidant. The listing below can also be followed to prepare your fruit.

ANTIOXIDANT PRETREATMENTS

Ascorbic acid:
1. 1/2 tsp per quart
2. 1/2 tsp per 2 cups granulated sugar
3. 1/2 tsp in 1 cup to 1 quart water, for dipping
fruit after peeling
4. 1/4 to 1/2 tsp to each quart sliced fruit,
dissolve in a little water and sprinkle on fruit
5. 1 TB citric acid and 1 tsp ascorbic acid to 1
gallon water for dipping fruit.

Lemon juice undiluted:
1. 2 TB juice over 1 quart fruit
2. 2 to 3 TB juice to 1 gallon water, for dipping
fruit

Citric acid:
1. 1 tsp. to 1 gallon water for dipping fruit
2. 1 TB citric acid to 1 gallon water for dipping
fruit

Vinegar and salt:
1. 2 TB salt and 2 TB vinegar in 1 gallon water
for holding fruit briefly, not more than 20
minutes, rinse before packing

Fruit Fresh:
Is a commercial pretreatment. Follow directions
on package.

THE BOILING BATH PROCESS FOR FRUIT

The following are easy to follow steps for using the boiling water bath process for canning fruit. If fruits are properly prepared and processed using the boiling water bath method, the canned fruits should be free of damaging bacteria, molds, and yeasts.

Here are steps including those discussed earlier in this chapter.

1. After the fruit is prepared for packing and the canning jars are heated, place the rack in the water bath canner. Put the canner on the stove, and fill the canner with 4 to 5 inches of warm water. If using raw pack method, turn the heat so the water temperature stays hot. If the hot pack method is used, bring water to a boil.

2. Pack the prepared fruit in jars one at a time following the recipe for each fruit.

3. Cover the packed fruit with its own syrup or juice from the kettle. Or use water or pickling solution if appropriate. Make sure the liquid is hot before pouring into heated jars, and leave the recommended head space.

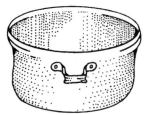

CANNING STEPS REVIEWED

Following is an overview of the steps for canning.   It includes steps discussed earlier in this   chapter.

1.   After the fruit is prepared for packing and the canning jars are heated, place the rack in the water bath canner.   Put canner on the stove and fill to 4 or 5 inches with warm water. If using raw pack,   heat so water temperature stays hot. For the hot pack method bring water to a boil.

2.   Pack the prepared fruit in jars one at time. Follow recipe for each fruit.

3.   Cover the packed fruit with its own syrup or juice from the kettle, water, or pickling solution. Make sure the liquid is hot before pouring into heated jars.   Leave recommended head space.

4.   Release air bubbles with a non-metal spatula. Add more hot liquid to maintain proper head space if needed.

5.   Wipe any food from rim and threads of jar.

6.   Apply jar closures to jars.

7.   Place jar in the canner and begin packing the next jar.

8.   After all of the jars have been completed and placed in the canner, pour hot water into the canner so the water level is 1 to 2 inches above the jar lids. Do not pour the water directly on the glass jars because they could shatter. Once water level is correct, close the canner.

9. Turn up the heat to bring the water in the canner to a boil. Begin counting the processing time when the water comes to a boil. The water should remain a constant boil of 212 degree F. throughout processing.

10. Occasionally check the water level to make sure at least 1 inch of water is above jar lids at all times. If you need to add water, always pour in boiling water. If the water is too cool, it could shatter the glass jars.

11. Process the jars by following the processing time directions called for in the recipe for the fruit you are canning.

12. Turn the heat off after the canner processing time is completed. Remove the jars and place them upright on a towel or rack to cool.

13. Let jars cool at room temperature in a draft free area.

14. After the jars have cooled for 12 to 24 hours, inspect them to make sure they have sealed.

15. Remove screw bands if using the two piece screw band and self sealing flat lid closures.

16. Test for leakage by turning jar on its side and rotating it slowly. If no leakage is present the jar has been sealed.

17. Label the jars and place the canned food in a storage area that is cool, dark and dry.

PRESSURE CANNING VEGETABLES

Vegetables may only be processed in a pressure canner. The boiling water bath should not be used for vegetables. It is true that people have processed vegetables in boiling water bath but they risk contacting botulism. The boiling water bath is not appropriate because the C. botulinum spores, which make toxins, can survive boiling at 212 degrees F. for over 5 hours. So, the only way to can low acid vegetables is to use pressure canners.

The processing steps for vegetables is the same as fruit, other than the fact that its mandatory to process vegetables with a pressure canner. In addition, the vegetables need to be pretreated by steam, microwave or boil blanching. (see discussion of blanching methods in first chapter)

For canning purposes, blanching by boiling is the preferred method because nutrients that are leeched out by the water are saved when the water is poured back into the jars as canning liquid.

After the vegetables have been stored for a length of time and you are ready to serve them, we recommend a step to make sure the toxins have been destroyed. Boil the vegetables vigorously for 15 to 20 minutes before eating them.

Stir the vegetables to make sure all pieces are thoroughly boiled. Greens and corn should be boiled at least 20 minutes.

If the food smells foul or foams up, it should be destroyed in a manner so people or animals will not accidently eat it.

Below are drying times for almost all foods, including Beef Jerky when using your Ronco Electric Food Dehydrator. This supersedes the information in the red Ronco instruction book. All foods should be sliced 1/8 inch or less to coincide with drying times below. Drying times can vary due to thickness of food and outside temperature.

DRYING TIMES

# Trays	Times	Vent Settings
1-3 trays	24-36 Hours	Top & Bottom Vents Fully Open
4-5 Trays	36-48 Hours	Top & Bottom Vents Fully Open
6-7 Trays	48-60 Hours	Top 3/4 Open(#3) Bottom Vent Fully Open

ROTATION OF TRAYS

To insure even drying, it is recommended that the Ronco Electric Food Dehydrator trays be rotated from top to bottom as well as a half turn to each tray to the left or right.

REMEMBER - Turn trays 180 degrees or half a turn to the left or right after rotating them up or down.

1 TO 5 TRAYS - Rotate trays top to bottom after approximately 12 hours.

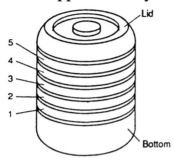 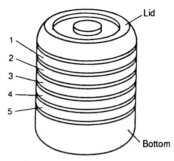

Before Trays are Moved   **After Trays are Moved**

6 TO 7 TRAYS- Rotate trays top to bottom at approximately 18 hours. Rotate trays in middle of dehydrator to bottom at approximately 36 hours.

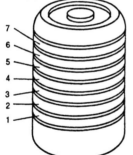 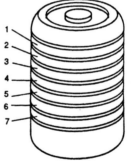

Before Trays are Moved   **18 Hours**
                                1st Tray Rotation

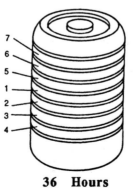

36 Hours
2nd Tray Rotation

Thinking about starting your own business?

Ronco Electric Dehydrator inspires successful gourmet beef jerky business

You can start your own business using your Food Dehydrator recipes and other products or crafts. Cindy Adair did. She purchased a Ronco Electric Food Dehydrator and started making her own beef jerky.

As she made it, she shared it with her co-workers, family and friends. "Everybody kept asking for more and I couldn't keep up with demand" said Cindy, so she bought a dozen more Ronco Dehydrators. Word spread quickly from that point and soon the Hawaiian Jungle Jerky company was born.

Anyone can enjoy making great, quality products like beef jerky with the Ronco Dehydrator. Cindy Adair of Hawaiian Jungle Jerky says, "I know it's true, I've got a company to prove it and I'm proud of it!"

Let your Ronco Electric Food Dehydrator inspire your business ideas.

It's easy to use your dehydrator to make meat jerkies, fruit snacks, potpourri or dried flower crafts and a lot more. The possibilities are only limited by your imagination.

Recipes Wanted

Do you have a recipe or use for the Ronco Electric Food Dehydrator that your family and friends are crazy about?

If you do, we'd like to hear from you. And if your recipe is selected for one of our upcoming publications, we will send you a special gift.

Send your recipes to:
Dehydrator Products
P.O. Box 4120
Carlsbad, CA 92018